Bourchier Wrey Savile

The Neanderthal skull on evolution

With three illustrations

Bourchier Wrey Savile

The Neanderthal skull on evolution
With three illustrations

ISBN/EAN: 9783337303488

Printed in Europe, USA, Canada, Australia, Japan

Cover: Foto ©Andreas Hilbeck / pixelio.de

More available books at **www.hansebooks.com**

THE

NEANDERTHAL SKULL

ON

Evolution,

IN

AN ADDRESS SUPPOSED TO BE DELIVERED

A.D. 2085.

WITH THREE ILLUSTRATIONS.

BY THE

Rev. BOURCHIER WREY SAVILE, M.A.,

RECTOR OF SHILLINGFORD, EXETER;
AUTHOR OF "THE TRUTH OF THE BIBLE."

"Man is descended from a hairy quadruped, furnished with a tail and pointed ears."—*Charles Darwin.*

"Without any doubt a long series of extinct worms were our direct ancestors." —*Professor Haeckel.*

"We cannot pronounce it a conquest of science, that man descends from the ape or any other animal whatever."—*Professor Virchow.*

LONDON:

LONGMANS AND CO.

—

1885.

CONTENTS.

ILLUSTRATIONS.

PREFACE.

THERE is no doubt that a great diversity of opinion respecting the doctrine of Evolution has been entertained by many eminent men for many ages. The Book of Job—which is probably the oldest book in the world, or as old as the Prisse papyrus in the Louvre, which claims an antiquity of 4000 years—may be dated about 2000 B.C. from the internal evidence, which speaks of the Pyramids (rendered in our English Bible as "desolate places," Job iii. 14) as the burial places of kings; and Egyptology teaches us that the practice of utilising Pyramids in that way ended with the sixth dynasty, which terminated some time before Abraham went down to Egypt. According to some Job is supposed to speak of one of our ancestors of the quadrupedal order when he says, "Vain man would be

wise, though man be born a wild ass's colt"
(ch. xi. 12). The Authorized Version introduces the word "like," but it is not
in the original; and therefore we must
accept the teaching of the Hebrew, which
shows that man is born " a wild ass," and
therefore supports the Darwinian theory;
though many will confidently assert that
another explanation or interpretation is
possible and more probable.

Thus the illustrious author of *Hamlet*, by
whatever name he is called, writing between
three and four thousand years after Job,
puts into the mouth of Ophelia this wise
sentiment—"We know what we are; but
know not what we may be." But this seems
to be contradicted by another eminent man
of our own time, as Thomas Carlyle
relates how John Sterling taught as
follows—"I affirm we do know whence
we come, and whither we go." Which
idea has been capped by another notabi-
lity of the 19th century, the late Lord
Beaconsfield, who in the best of his
novels, entitled *Tancred* (Anthony Trollope

classes Thackeray as the best of that style
of writers, and Disraeli as the worst), puts
into the mouth of one of his ideal
characters—a blue-stocking lady—the following Darwinian dictum—"We were
fishes, we shall be crows; we had fins, we
may have wings."

This, however, has been plainly contradicted by one of the most eminent *savans*
of modern times, the very learned Agassiz,
an honour and an ornament to the land
both of his birth and adoption, who
declares that the Transmutation theory
of one species to another is "wholly
without foundation in fact." And so in
his *Travels in Brazil*, when speaking of the
Evolution hypothesis, he very plainly
declares that "The theory is a scientific
blunder; untrue in its facts, unscientific in
its method, and ruinous in its tendency."

Who shall decide when doctors differ so much, as we have already seen by
a reference to the opinions expressed by
certain notabilities of various ages, from
Job to Agassiz, embracing the tolerably

long period of 4000 years? Hence we
have endeavoured to let each man have
his own say, and speak for himself, by
collecting together in one focus the opinions of almost all the celebrities of the
18th and 19th centuries on the subject of
EVOLUTION, as set forth in an address,
supposed to be delivered by the Neanderthal Skull two centuries hence, when, to
use the expressive words of Professor
Tyndall, all the men and women of this
fast and progressive age will "have melted
into the infinite azure of the past."

Some years ago I had the privilege of
exchanging works with Professor Tyndall,
in which business I always found him
kind, courteous and obliging. On one
occasion I ventured to ask him this
question—"If Mr. Darwin's theory be
true, that MAN is descended from the
larvæ of an ascidian born of an egg, how
was the first infant mammal nourished
and fed, on the supposition that its immediate ancestor was a non-mammal?"
Although I assured my distinguished

correspondent that the question was asked in no captious spirit, but with a real desire for information, I could obtain no response to my enquiry. I was therefore fain to let the matter drop, naturally concluding that if so eminent a scientist as Professor Tyndall was unwilling to answer so plain a question, the theory was not likely to be true.

After an interval of some years, I had an opportunity of asking the same question of Mr. Darwin himself, through the circumstance of his son and my son-in-law being brother-officers in the Royal Engineers; when he was kind enough to reply to my question without delay. After a brief correspondence, I give his final letter, which was written about a year before his lamented death, and which reads as follows :—

"Down, Beckenham, Kent, Oct. 1, 1881.

"Dear Sir,—The secretary tubules in the mammery glands are generally admitted to be of the same nature or homologous with the glands over the whole skin. Even with mammals there is some gradation in perfection as in the mammery

glands; and in *Echidna* the young suck off the
surface of the skin the secreted milk, for there is no
nipple.

"In the case of certain fish, the ova are hatched
in a marsupial sack on the surface of the stomach of
the male, and the young, when hatched, feed on the
mucus secreted from the skin lining the sack;
and here, as I believe, we see what might be the
commencement of a simple mammery gland, as in
Echidna, etc. This is, of course, *only an hypothesis.*
The exact steps in the Evolutionary process could be
discovered *only* by the observation of *animals which
became extinct during the earliest part of the secondary
period.*

"Dear Sir, yours faithfully,
"CHARLES DARWIN."

We may fairly infer from this letter,
that the distinguished founder of what is
populary known as "The Darwinian
Theory" acknowledged in the maturity
of his age and fame—first, that it was
"only an hypothesis;" and secondly,
that the exact steps in the Evolutionary
process could *only* be discovered by the
observation of animals which had become
extinct ages ago, which seems like admitting that it never could or would be
proved.

Professor Tyndall has well said, when alluding to mere theories, another name for "only an hypothesis," that "without verification, a theoretic conception is a mere figment of the intellect." * And the recently, but most deservedly "titled" Sir Richard Owen has said, that "observation of the actual change of any one species into another, through any or all of the hypothesised transmuting influences, *has not yet been recorded.*" Hence the force of Dr. Elam's syllogism respecting hypotheses and theoretic conceptions: "The theory," he argues, " of Organic Evolution is an unverified theoretic conception. Therefore, *Organic Evolution is a mere figment of the intellect.*"

Without seeking to lessen the deservedly high reputation of the late Mr. Darwin, one of the most eminent Naturalists of the 19th century, and who treated religion in a very different spirit from that adopted

---

* *Fragments of Science,* by John Tyndall, F.R.S., p. 469 ; fifth edition.

by many of his disciples, it is surprising
to observe the extravagant praise which
some of them have used towards the
master, possibly with the hope and expectation that his great name might be
conveniently used to cover their more
advanced speculative theories. Thus at
the time of the late Mr. Darwin's lamented
death, the *Western Morning News* confidently
asserted that he was to be ranked as one
of the three greatest teachers of science
which the world has ever seen. *Bacon*
ranked as the first, *Newton* as the second,
and *Darwin* as the third. I trust I shall
not be deemed irreverent, if I say that
such a comparison and such an order of
merit, reminds me of an American writer
who published a work entitled " Sands of
Gold, or the wisest sayings of *Solomon,
Shakespeare* and *Martin Tupper.*" In
similar strains Professor Huxley compared
Darwin to Aristotle * and Newton, while

---

* Professor Huxley compares Mr. Darwin to
Aristotle, which may be accounted for thus. Darwin's observations on his various theories are

declaring that "his intellect had no superior." Although comparisons are proverbially odious, many cultured persons would prefer the opinion of Professor Owen, the first scientist of the present time, when he pronounced the celebrated French Naturalist Cuvier "the greatest man since Aristotle, not to be repeated for 2000 years." * And when Professor Huxley speaks of Darwin's unproved theoretic conception of man having been evolved from the larvæ of an ascidian tadpole as "an established truth,"† or as Mr. Ball, ‡ the Astronomer Royal for Ireland, calls it, " a necessary truth," I am reminded that Professor Huxley's opinions are somewhat unstable on this subject, as

---

continually made to depend on the force of the word "probable." And Aristotle in his *Poetics* says— "This, too, is *probable*, according to a saying of Agathon: 'It is a part of *probability* that many improbable things will happen.'"

* *Journals and Letters of Caroline Fox*, vol. i., pp. 261, 262.

† Huxley's *Lay Sermons*, p. 295.

‡ Article in *Longman's Magazine*, Nov. 1883, p. 77.

in another place he admits that Darwin's
theory is only " an hypothesis," adding,
" After much consideration, and assuredly
with no bias against Mr. Darwin's views,
it is our clear conviction that as the
evidence stands, it is not absolutely *proven*
that a group of animals............has ever
been originated by selection, whether
artificial or natural."

More just and more discriminating
is Professor Tyndall's eulogy of Mr.
Darwin's powers as an investigator of
natural and scientific truth, while at the
same time he is convinced that some day
Mr. Darwin's hypothesis and theoretic
conceptions will " undergo modifications,"
referring, I conclude, to those who more
or less ignore the dogmatic teaching of
Scripture on the subject.

" If Darwin," says the professor, " rejects the notion of creative power acting
after human fashion, it is certainly not
because he is unacquainted with the
numberless exquisite adaptations, on which
this notion of a supernatural Artificer has

been founded. His book is a repository of
the most startling facts of this description.
......It is the mind thus stored with the
choicest materials of the teleologist that
rejects teleology, seeking to refer these
wonders to natural causes. They illustrate, according to him, the method of
nature, not the 'technic' of a manlike
Artificer."*

It is difficult to imagine how any one
who rejects "Teleology," or the Argument from Design, and accepts a Supreme
Creator, as we rejoice to know the late
Mr. Darwin cordially did during his
honoured lifetime, can explain, *e.g.*, the
formation of *the carboniferous era* in the
geological strata in which it is found,
and its adaptation for the *exclusive* use of
man ; or the peculiar nature of *the hive-bee*,
which has been so ably interpreted by
Professor Tyndall in his Belfast Address ;
or the wonderful and complex structure of

---

* Tyndall's "Belfast Address," in *Fragments of
Science*, p. 511.

the human eye. On this last point, the learned German Helmholtz, as the late Professor Clifford boasted in an address to the British Association in 1872, has declared that—"If an optician sent me a human eye as an instrument, I should send it back to him with grave reproaches for the carelessness of his work, and demand back my money; "*—but this bold avowal of Atheism, which must sincerely pain every one who has the slightest regard for the God of Revelation, neither disproves the inference to be drawn from teleology, nor the existence of a Supreme Creator.

Now it is somewhat remarkable that Mr. Darwin himself, in distinct opposition to the opinion of Helmholtz, very candidly says—"To suppose that *the eye*, with all its immutable contrivances for adjusting the focus to different distances, for admitting different amounts of light, and for

---

* *Lectures and Essays,* by the late W. K. Clifford, F.R.S., vol. i., p. 145.

the correction of spherical and chromatic aberration, could have been formed by ' Natural Selection,' seems, I freely confess, *absurd in the highest possible degree*............
If it could be demonstrated that any complex organ existed, which could not possibly have been by numerous successive, slight modifications, my theory would *absolutely break down.*" *

A remarkable incident connected with the eye has been recently recorded, which confirms the belief so frankly expressed by Mr. Darwin, that to imagine so exquisitely formed an instrument of men and animals is due to " Natural Selection," and not to the Divine Artificer, is " absurd in the highest possible degree." The *Detroit News*, U.S., mentions the case of a young man, 19 years of age, who had been totally blind for many years, owing to an inflammation, which caused the lower lid of each eye to grow up over the ball and pupil. A distinguished oculist de-

---

* Darwin's *Origin of Species*, p. 189.

b 4

clared that the only way to cure him was
to cut away the overgrown lid. In doing
this, the mucous membrane necessarily came
away with it, leaving the eyeball unpro-
tected. The patient was placed under the
influence of chloroform, and *the mucous
membrane from the eye of a rabbit* was
procured, and placed over the ball of the
patient's eye. The operation so far has
been entirely successful, and after the
patient has recovered strength, the other
eye is to be operated upon in a similar
manner. The transplanting of the membrane from the eye of an animal to that
of a human being has been successfully
performed only on rare occasions. And it
is worthy of note that the loss of the
membrane in this instance could not have
been supplied either by the Natural Selection theory, or by the skill of the cleverest
optician that ever lived. Hence in supply-
ing this delicate covering it was necessary
to use *the handiwork of God*, as found in
another creature's eye, as formed by the
Omnipotent Artificer of the universe.

Hence, in the spiritual application of such important truths, we read of the God of revelation commanding His people to "anoint thine eyes with eye-salve, that thou mayest see" (Rev. iii. 18).

Many scientific men consider that the attempt to support the doctrine of "Evolution" by the theory of *Natural Selection* has completely "broken down." Hence, says Dr. Elam, in his *Gospel of Evolution*, "Natural Selection is merely an euphemism for a negation—a happy phrase for something that has no existence. In itself it is *nothing;* in its application to the explanation of development of structure and function, it is full of irreconcilable contradictions and incoherences. This ought to be sufficient, but there are other and even weightier objections. If Natural Selection were a real agency, two definite consequences ought inevitably to result. First, we ought to meet with frequent, if not constant, evidences of transition, so numerous and so various, that all 'organized beings would be blended together in an *inextricable chaos.'* And secondly, we ought to observe a slow and gradual, but perceptible improvement in species generally, especially marked in those whose generations succeed each other rapidly. *Neither of these is observable.*"*

There are upwards of 20,000 species of animals in creation, and all experience shows that in every instance when crossing species has been attempted, in place of there being any improvement, or the transmutation of one species into another, *sterility* has been the invariable result. So that it seems contrary to observation and experience to assume that there ever was a time when this invariable law was reversed. Dr. Carruthers, an eminent botanist, has declared that "*No single case of Evolution of one species from another has come within the observation of man.*"

Hence, Professor Huxley justly ob-

---

* See Dr. Elam's article in *The Contemporary Review* of 1880. The phrase "inextricable chaos," is used by Mr. Darwin in his *Origin of Species*, p. 407.

serves that "the methods of all sciences are—1. Observation of facts; 2. Comparison and Classification; 3. Deduction; 4. Verification;"* and we have already seen in respect to the first and last of these rules that the observation of facts is dead against the Evolution theory; for notwithstanding frequent challenges the supporters of the theory have never succeeded in observing a single instance, in all the millions of years invented in its support, of one species of animal life turning into another. And as for verification, the syllogistic reasoning already quoted of Dr. Elam seems unanswerable, as he acutely says—

"Without verification, a theoretic conception is a mere figment of the intellect.

"The theory of Organic Evolution is an unverified theoretic conception.

"Therefore ORGANIC EVOLUTION is a mere figment of the intellect." †

---

* Huxley's *Lay Sermons*, p. 92.

† Dr. Elam's "Gospel of Evolution," in *Contemporary Review* of 1880.

Thoroughly convinced of the soundness of this syllogism as propounded by Dr. Elam respecting the Evolution hypothesis, as being "a mere figment of the intellect," and therefore untrue, I have nevertheless spoken of the late Mr. Charles Darwin throughout the following treatise with sincere respect, as one of the greatest Naturalists of our time, though unable to place him on a par, as Professor Huxley has done, with Newton; who, as most people admit, possessed a greater genius and displayed more mental power than any other of the sons of men. And this is to be seen more clearly in the profound reverence which the immortal Sir Isaac entertained for the God of revelation, as well as in his Christian humility, so clearly manifested in his memorable saying, "I do not know what I may appear to the world, but to myself I seem to have been only like a boy playing on the sea-shore, and diverting myself in now and then finding a smoother pebble or a prettier shell than ordinary, whilst the great Ocean of Truth

lay all undiscovered before me." * Which
drew from Pope the famous eulogium—

"Nature and Nature's laws lay hid in night,
God said, 'Let Newton be,' and all was light."

Mr. Darwin's just fame will rest upon
the charm of his writings, the depth of his
researches, and the mass of information
which he had accumulated; nor will it be
lessened by his approval of Christian
Missions, and the regard which he ever
manifested for the religious principles of
others, in striking contrast to the outspoken
and materialistic atheism of some who
claimed to be his disciples.

I have therefore endeavoured to show—

1st. That the Evolution theory is "only
an hypothesis" according to Mr. Darwin's
own admission; and therefore Dr. Elam's
description of it is just, when he terms it
" an unverified theoretic conception."

2nd. That this theory conflicts with the

* Brewster's *Life of Newton*, vol. ii., p. 407. Sir
David justly remarks, "This memorable and noble
sentiment was uttered a short time before his death."

infallible Word of Truth, as the language of
Moses in the first chapter of Genesis plainly
contradicts the assertion of man having
been developed from the lower animals;
and declares that man came into existence
by the sole act of creative power on the
part of an Omnipotent Being, who determined to form man of the dust of the ground
in His own image, after His own likeness.
" So God created man; male and female
created He them."

3rd. That it is a grievous mistake to
suppose, what is often asserted with surprising confidence, that *all* the learned
men, as Sir Joseph Hooker thought, had
accepted the doctrine of " EVOLUTION."   I
have shown, on the contrary, by quoting the
ipssissima verba, that almost all the scientific celebrities of the 19th century have
rejected the *Evolutionary theory*, either
positively or inferentially. Even Professor
Tyndall, who has spoken in deservedly
high terms of Mr. Darwin, considers it
" certain " that his (Darwin's) theory of
Evolution will undergo " modifications."

Are we not, therefore, warranted in supposing, as I have ventured to predict, that before many years have elapsed this hypothesis, like other speculations of an unsubstantial nature, will have disappeared like a mist before the rising sun.

If any thing could convince me of the possibility of the Evolution theory being true, it would be an interesting and valuable work by Mrs. F. J. Hughes, the widow of a clergyman, and I believe a relative of the late Mr. Darwin, entitled, *Harmonies of Tones and Colours Developed by Evolution.* It is written, apparently, in support of the Darwinian theory, with all that grace and gentleness which is so becoming and peculiar to the better sex, when engaged on subjects of heated controversy, as well as in a spirit of sincere Christian devotion. But it is evident that a scientific knowledge of "thorough bass" can alone enable the reader to follow the train of thought adopted by Mrs. Hughes in her clever and unpretending work.

While, therefore, compelled to dissent

from her conclusions, I gladly rest upon one of the mottoes which she has prefixed to her work—" Search the Scriptures. . . . they are they which testify of ME." While I exceedingly admire the whole " get up " of the work in question, the beauty of the type, with its illustrative coloured diagrams, and the delightful spirit in which the work is composed, I am content to adhere to my previous opinion that the origin of the human race on earth is due solely and exclusively to the last act of Divine Wisdom, in creating man after the image and likeness of God; and that this feeling is in a great measure shared by Mrs. Hughes herself I cannot doubt, from the fact of her DEDICATION having been addressed " to those searchers after truth, who, without implicit trust in their own finite powers, take delight in tracing the deep laws of the Almighty as typified in His word, and embodied in the beautiful work of Nature."

One more testimony I venture to give on this interesting subject, from the pen of,

possibly, the most gifted writer of fiction
that the world has ever seen. Some hitherto
unpublished letters of the late Mrs. Cross
(known to the world as " George Eliot,")
have recently (March, 1884) been commented on in the *Journal des Débats*, by
M. James Darmester, which have been
placed in his hands by a correspondent of
the great authoress. In one, bearing date
Dec. 5th, 1859, after reading Darwin's
Origin of Species, George Eliot writes, with
that clear grasp of truth and that charming
grace for which this gifted lady was so
celebrated—" So the world gets on step by
step to brave clearness and honesty. But
the chain of Darwinism, and all the ex-
planations of the march by which things
have been produced, *make but a feeble impression upon me, compared with the mystery
lying beneath this same march.*" Hence, we
are not surprised at her hearty condemnation of the scepticism and Latitudinarianism
which prevails with so many inferior
minds in the present day. In a letter
dated Nov. 26th, 1862, she writes—" I am

too deeply convinced of the efficacy of all sincere belief, and of the moral aridity which follows the loss of it, to have any thing in me of the negative propagandist. In fact, I *have very little sympathy with the class of Freethinkers, and I have lost all interest in merely anti-religious polemics.*"

From the life of this highly-gifted lady, published in 1883, under the title of *George Eliot: A Critical Study of her Life, Writings and Philosophy*, by G. W. Cooke, I should imagine a very happy change must have come over her towards the close of her career, relative to the principles of the Freethinkers, very different from those she must have entertained in early life, when Assistant Editor of the *Westminster Review ;* as the differences between the principles of the Free-thinking school and the ordinary view of the great body of professing Christians on the doctrine of "Evolution" and other cognate subjects, may be summarily expressed as follows :—

1. With regard to the *Origin of Man—*

Was it by Creation or Evolution, not as propounded by Mr. Darwin, but as set forth by Professor Haeckel, to the extent of dead · matter being capable of evolving organic life ?

2.. Is the Mosaic Cosmogony, as recorded in the first chapter of Genesis, or are the early Cosmogonies of those who were without a revelation from on high, the most like what we now know to be truth as the result of modern scientific discovery ?—*e.g.*, Which is true, the Ptolemaic system of the ancients, or the Copernican system of the moderns ? Do the ancient Cosmogonies, such as that of the *Egyptians*, who traced the origin of the universe to "*the Egg* of the great Cackler ; " or that of the *Phœnicians*, who considered " *Mud* " to be the origin ; or the *Chaldœans*, who pronounced in favour of " *Chaos ;* " or the learned *Grecians*, who, according to Empedocles, named "the four elements" of *Fire, Air, Water* and *Earth*, as the original creator of all things ?—I ask if such doctrines are to be believed, in preference to the calm and philosophic statement of Scripture, which reveals one Supreme Omnipotent Being as the Creator of all?

3. Is the *Origin of Life* to be credited to this Supreme Omnipotent Creator, or to a fortuitous concourse of *atoms*, as some of the Agnostic philosophers of the 19th century contend?

4. Is the *antiquity of man* to be dated *circa* 6,000 years ago, as Scripture teaches? and which satisfied the enlarged mind of Cuvier, the most profound scientist, according to the testimony of Owen, since the time of Aristotle? or must we accept the wild speculations of such men as Professor Waitz, who gives men an antiquity of 135,000 million years, or of Professor Huxley, who considers that is not near long enough?!!!

5. Is *Teleology*, or the arguments from design, to be accepted as seen, *e.g.*, in the formation of the Carboniferous era for the exclusive use of man, or in the mathematical instincts of the bee, or the exquisite formation of the human eye?

Are these, and a multitude of other things, to be accepted in proof of a Divine Creator, who loves the work of His own hands, or are they to be entirely ignored ?

6. Is the doctrine of the *Unity of Race* to be accepted according to the teaching of Scripture, or are we to prefer the speculation of Professor Huxley, who declares he does not know one single scientific person who believes it ?

7. Was man created originally *perfect*, though in many instances fallen to a savage state ? or has he been developed from a *savage monkey* into a civilized intellectual man, such as Bacon, or Milton, or Newton ? *

---

* The building of the Great Pyramid of Ghizeh, which was erected certainly within three centuries after Noah and his family emerged from the Ark, together with the contemporary statue of Pharaoh " Chephren," which Piazzi Smyth has justly described as "the earliest statue in the world, and the most solemn and monarch-like figure that has ever been produced in stone," is a sufficient answer to the theory of cultured man being a developed savage. See P. Smyth's *Life and Work at the Great Pyramid*, vol. i., pp. 13—15, for an animated account of this beautiful statue.

These are questions which are now engaging the attention of the learned at the present time. In the following treatise, an attempt is made to answer the first of them, while slightly glancing at some of the others, with a sincere prayer and a hope, that we may arrive at the true and just conclusion.

B. W. S.

P.S. Since writing the above, I have been asked more than once for my opinion of a very remarkble work, which treats of the Evolutionary theory, entitled *Natural Law in the Spiritual World*, by Henry Drummond, F.R.S.E., F.G.S.; and which has attained great popularity, as may be judged from the fact, that within the year of its publication (1884) it had reached the "thirteenth edition, completing the twenty-ninth thousand," as is stated on the title-page of the copy now before me.

Though at the time unable to give any answer, from the simple fact of not having

then seen the work in question, I received
a letter from a friend—of whose judgment
I entertain great respect—an elderly
Evangelical clergyman, who had taken a
high degree at Oxford half a century ago,
and whose opinion of the work in question was thus expressed—"I have read
with interest and pleasure Drummond's
Natural Law, &c., and think the chapters
on *Biogenesis*, *Environment*, *Semi-Parasitism* and *Parasitism*, suggestive of much
truth and practical instruction."

Ten days later I received unexpectedly
from a stranger the present of a small
work, entitled, *Remarks on Drummond's
"Natural Law*," by Benjamin Wills Newton, who was formerly a "Fellow of
Exeter College, Oxford." The kind
donor, after eulogising the *Remarks* as
containing "a clearer exposition of Scripture than any work with which he was
acquainted," warns me not "to be pre-
judiced by the dogmatic tone of the author,
which is sometimes apt to excite a feeling
of opposition to the view he advocates."

c

The first thing which struck me on looking into the *Remarks* was, that though at the commencement Mr. Newton avowed his intention of not giving "an analysis of Mr. Drummond's book, or to argue philosophically against it, but simply to quote certain passages, and ask you (the reader) to test them by the Word of God, and so form your own judgment "—he expresses his great surprise at Mr. Drummond's work having been "widely circulated and *widely welcomed, even by Evangelical Christians*" (pp. 3, 4).

Moreover, Mr. Newton quotes, with apparent pleasure, an extract from the *Guardian* review of *Natural Law in the Spiritual World*, to the following effect—"The extravagant praises which have been lavished on this book have blinded men to the fact that the Christianity which fits in so conveniently with Mr. Drummond's scientific framework, is *not the Christianity of the Bible or of the Catholic Church.*" To make this closing sentence objectively true, the *Guardian*

reviewer should have prefixed "Christianity" by the term "Sacerdotal," and
"Catholic" by the distinctive epithet
"Roman." For it must be manifest to
all that the Christianity of the New Testament, as explained by St Paul, and that
taught by the Church of Rome during the
last thirteen centuries, is as distinct as the
Catholicity of the primitive Christians
differs from that of the Papal Church in
the present day.

That Professor Drummond rates the
Church of Rome at its proper value may
be inferred from the following passage:—
"No more perfect or more sad example,"
he says, "of semi-parasitism exists, than
in the case of those illiterate thousands
who, scattered everywhere throughout the
habitable globe, swell the lower ranks
of the Church of Rome. Had an organi-
sation been specially designed, indeed,
to induce the parasitic habit in the souls
of men, nothing better to its disastrous
end could be established than the system
of Roman Catholicism. Roman Catho-

licism offers to the masses a molluscan shell............An assurance of salvation at the smallest possible cost forms the tempting bait held out to a conscience-stricken world by the Romish Church. Thousands, therefore, who have never been taught to use their faculties in 'working out their own salvation,' thousands who will not exercise themselves religiously, and who yet cannot be without the exercises of religion, entrust themselves in idle faith to *that venerable house of refuge which for centuries has stood between God and man*" (pp. 327—8).

Again, Mr. Newton quotes, approvingly the assertion of the *Guardian* reviewer, when he says, " Mr. Drummond does not seem aware of all that his theory implies. For all the unregenerate it necessarily implies *annihilation*." To which Mr. Newton adds—" The reviewer *rightly* says that Mr. Drummond's book teaches *the annihilation of the unregenerate*" (p. 172). In opposition to these unjust conclusions of the *Guardian* and Mr. Newton, let us

hear what Professor Drummond really
teaches on this subject—"Should any one
object, that from this scientific standpoint
the opposite of salvation is *annihilation*, the
answer is at hand.   From this standpoint
there is no such word.   Each man in the
silence of his own soul must 'work out
this salvation for himself with fear and
trembling '—with fear, realizing the momentous issues of his task; with trembling,
lest before the tardy work be done, the
voice of Death should summon him to
stop" (pp. 118, 119).

Again, hear Professor Drummond declaring—

"Hitherto the Christian philosopher has
remained content with *the Scientific Evidence against Annihilation*......For the first
time Science touches Christianity positively on the doctrine of Immortality.   It
confronts us with an actual definition of
Eternal Life, based on a full and rigidly
accurate examination of the necessary
conditions.   Science does not pretend that
it can fulfil these conditions.   Its votaries

make no claim to possess the Eternal Life" (p. 205).

It is evident from these passages, that neither the *Guardian* reviewer nor Mr. B. W. Newton has a right conception of Professor Drummond's real teaching on the subject of "annihilation." It is true that we may without difficulty find passages in this work which contain either grave error, or we have sadly misunderstood the professor's meaning; *e.g.*, when he commits himself to the startling statement, apparently put forth in order to support the teaching of Mr. Herbert Spencer—that "for eighteen hundred years only one definition of *Life Eternal* was before the world." *Now there are two* (p. 203)—Mr. Drummond can scarcely feel surprised at being considered by some an accomplished Agnostic. Or when he speaks of the grand doctrine of the "ATONEMENT" in so imperfect and unsatisfactory a manner, as he has done (see p. 335, &c.), though carefully guarded by the omnipotent "if," he has laid himself open to the charge, which we know one writer brings against him, though we deem the charge doubtful, of making " a declaration that a Unitarian might endorse."

Or when he speaks in such contemptuous tones of the sudden conversion of " a blackguard picked from the streets" (p. 331), he has exposed himself to the just retort of an able critic of his rash words— " This is monstrous. As to ' blackguards of the streets,' one might almost quote the words of Christ, ' *The publicans and the harlots go into the kingdom of heaven before you;*' and those other like words of His inspired Apostle, ' *Not many wise men after the flesh are called.*' "

Let me, however, mention other instances where the learned professor has been evidently misunderstood, as, *e.g.*—

1. Those who are well read in the scientific literature of the day, in reference to what is termed " spontaneous generation," cannot but feel (as regards the controversy which was carried on in the *Nineteenth Century*, at the beginning of

1878, between Professor Tyndall and Dr. Bastian) that the theory was completely overthrown, and that it never would recover from the crushing blow which it then received. The theory was then " defeated along the whole line," as one Scientist admitted, and Professor Drummond justly says, that " the heresy of spontaneous generation is so thoroughly discredited now, that scarcely any authority will lend his name to it " (p. 88). Nevertheless, Mr. Drummond has stated the doctrine of " spontaneous generation " so incautiously, by writing, " A thousand modern pulpits every seventh day are preaching *the doctrine of spontaneous generation ;* it is the leading theology of the modern novel ; and much of the cultured writing of the day devotes itself to the earnest preaching of this Gospel "—that he must not be surprised if he were accused of believing it, just as he has been of holding the doctrine of annihilation ! ! ! (see pp. 61—67).

2. Mr. Newton, in his *Remarks* on the way in which Professor Drummond

has spoken, appears to consider him as nothing more or less than an avowed Materalist, an euphemistic expression for a rank Atheist. Mr. Newton more than once remarks upon the professor's expressions that "Matter is uncreatable and indestructible," and that "the atoms of which the visible universe is built up, bear distinct marks of being *manufactured* articles" (pp. 27, 189).

Mr. Newton admits that these statements may be so explained as not necessarily to deny the existence of the Creator, and the word "manufactured" may be applied to God as well as to man; so that to charge the professor with inculcating Atheism is a grievous misunderstanding of his creed. "When will it be seen," asks the professor, "that the characteristic of the Christian religion is its life—that a true Theology must begin with a Biology? Theology is the Science of God. When will men treat God as inorganic?" (p. 297).

3. On the chief subject of the work, viz., the doctrine of Evolution, Mr. Newton is

singularly unhappy and unjust in his treatment of Professor Drummond. His *Remarks* are thus worded—" Mr. Drummond is avowedly an Evolutionist. It is impossible to be an Evolutionist, and to believe that matter was created in the sense of being called into existence out of nothing. 'Evolution' is a word which by the force of its own intrinsic meaning *nullifies creation*. . . . Evolutionary Philosophy persists in maintaining that by Natural Law minerals are evolved into vegetables, beasts and men ; and maintains also that men are raised into spiritual being by a like operation of the *same* law that has evolved them from lower forms of existence " (pp. 124, 188).

Professor Drummond may have anticipated such an accusation as likely to be brought against him, since he virtually replies to this apparent charge of Atheism in the following words :—

" The inorganic world is staked off from the living world by barriers which have never yet been crossed from within. No

change of substance, no modification of
environment, no chemistry, no electricity
nor any Evolution can endow any single
atom of the mineral world with the
attribute of life" (pp. 6, 8).

"As the veil is lifted by Christianity, it
strikes men dumb with wonder. For the
goal of Evolution is Jesus Christ. The
Christian life is the only life that will
ever be completed. Apart from Christ, the
life of man is a broken pillar, the race of
men an unfinished pyramid. And when
Christ who is our life shall appear, then
shall we also appear with Him in glory"
(p. 314).

"If among the more recent revelations of
Nature there is one thing more significant
for religion than another, it is the majestic
spectacle of the rise of kingdoms towards
scarcer, yet nobler forms, and simpler, yet
diviner ends. Of the early stage, the first
development of the earth from the nebulous
matrix of space, *Science speaks with reserve.*
The second, the evolution of each individual from the simple protoplasmic cell to

the formed adult, is *proved*. The still
wider evolution, not of solitary individuals,
but of all the individuals within each
province—in the vegetable world, from the
unicellular cryptogam to the highest phane-
rogram; in the animal world, from the
amorphous amœba to MAN—*is at least sus-
pected*, the gradual rise of types being at
all events a fact. But now at last we see
kingdoms evolving. . . . And so out of the
infinite complexity there arises an infinite
simplicity, the foreshadowing of a final
unity of that—

"'One God, one law, one element,
    And one far off divine event,
    To which the whole creation moves'" (p. 412).

The great value of Professor Drummond's work on *Natural Law in the Spiritual
World*, is the noble stand which the author
has made on behalf of Evangelical teaching
as presented to us in the New Testament,
which pervades and permeates the work
throughout, from the first dawn of spritual
life when the heart is converted and the
new birth has taken place, until the time

when Christ next appears, and the believer, with a purified soul and a resurrection body, is caught up to meet the Saviour in the air, and so to be " for ever with the Lord." Let any unprejudiced disciple, who knows experimentally what St. Paul calls " the truth as it is in Jesus," carefully study the following pages of Professor Drummond's work ; and he will have a most valuable *repertoire* of the Pauline philosophy, as it appears in the various Epistles which the great Apostle wrote to the different Churches he had founded, under the direct inspiration of the Spirit of God. (See pp. 89, 104, 118, 135, 140, 145, 181, 169, 171-2, 176, 294, 309-10, 313-4, 336, 393-4.)

I know no work which has done such good service for the cause of Christ, notwithstanding its blemishes, in its endeavour, on the one hand, to uphold Evangelical teaching as manifested in the spiritual life of a converted soul; and on the other, to show the agreement between religion in its highest sense, and the doctrine of true science, as Professor Drum-

mond's *Natural Law in the Spiritual World*
has done. Happy would it be if all who
profess a love for the Scriptures and the
interests of science, could realize what
Dr. McCosh has so well said in his *Method
of the Divine Government.* " Science," he
observes, " has a foundation, and so has
Religion. Let them unite their foundations,
and the basis will be broader, and they
will be two compartments of one great
fabric reared to the glory of God. Let the
one be the outer and the other the inner
court.   In the one, let all look and admire
and adore ; and in the other, let those who
have faith kneel and pray and praise. Let
the one be the sanctuary, where human
learning may present its richest incense as
an offering to God ; and the other, the
holiest of all, separated from it by a vail
now rent in twain, and in which on a blood-
sprinkled mercy-seat, we pour out the love
of a reconciled heart, and hear the oracles
of the living God."

Although it is certain that never before
has real, true, genuine science achieved

such splendid results, as those which have
been brought to light in the 19th century,
of which we are receiving the benefit in the
present day; it is equally true, as it has
been forcibly remarked by a critic of Professor Haeckel's doctrines, that "Never
before have scientific men talked such unscientific nonsense, or promulgated such
baseless fallacies. It is the age of great
discoveries; but also the age of hasty ge-
neralisation, rash assertions, unwarranted
assumptions, and specious sophisms on the
part of the discoverers."

We think this may be seen in some of
the most recent utterances on the subject
of Evolution. Professor Huxley is reported to have said in a lecture, *On the
Origin of Man*, delivered at the Royal
Institution, April 9th, 1880, that "The
doctrine of Evolution was no longer a
matter of speculation, but *an absolute fact.*"
Or as Professor Fowler is said to have
expressed it, at the Reading Church Congress of 1883, that "Evolution was *a
certainty*, that man was evolved like other

animals; and that special creation of known forms could not be admitted."

Assuming that the dogmas of these two Professors are correctly reported, they appear to be under as complete a delusion, as a certain person, the bearer of one of the most illustrious names in English history, who has made himself very notorious of late years, and got into much trouble thereby, by continually thrusting his hobby before the public—to the effect that the Copernican system is all false— that Sir Isaac Newton was a great ignoramus, and that the earth we inhabit is as flat as a pancake! He has favoured the author of this book with many letters containing some surprising statements, assuring him that all the clergy of the Church of England are infidels, "save six." Poor man!

SHILLINGFORD RECTORY, EXETER,
January 1, 1885.

The Neanderthal Skull.

B

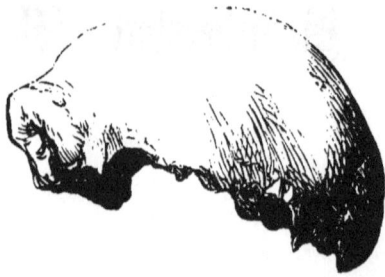

An exact copy of the Neanderthal Skull as exhibited at the meeting of the British Association in 1880.

An imaginary portrait of the supposed owner of the skull, which was handed round at that meeting.

The Neanderthal Skull.

METHOUGHT I was seated one summer evening of the year 2085, in St. James' Hall, Piccadilly. It was filled with a vast assemblage of people, amongst whom I recognised celebrities who had long passed away, as well as many who were still in the land of the living.

Suddenly the green curtain was drawn up, when I beheld in the middle of the stage a table, on which was placed a large charger, or dish, containing a skull, very like one seen at the Polytechnic Exhibition some years ago, when Professor Pepper appeared to make the head *minus* its trunk talk in the usual way.

An undefined sensation ran through the assembly; loud exclamations of surprise were uttered on all sides, in the midst of

B 2

which a voice exclaimed, " Why, it is the exact counterpart of the NEANDERTHAL SKULL!" on which another voice, apparently that of Professor Huxley, remarked, " It is the most ape-like skull I ever saw." I then recollected having read of a meeting of *savans* held at Bonn, in 1857, when this famous skull was produced, having been found not long before in a cave close to the village of Neanderthal. It then excited great interest in the scientific world, though many doubted whether it belonged to the simian or the human race. When it was exhibited by Professor Shafenhausen at the Swansea Meeting of the British Association in 1880, Professor Rolleston took the skull lovingly in his arms, and declared his unhesitating belief that it was not that of an ape nor of an idiot, but that of a savage man about 50 years of age, with a small brain, but well able to hold his own in the struggle for existence. And Carl Vögt, a strong partisan of the Atheistic development theory, acknowledged that one of his best friends, a man of great distinction, had precisely the same conformation of the occiput.

On the other hand, many supposed the Neanderthal skull to be either that of an intellectual ape of the highest order, or else the veritable missing link for which speculative *savans* have been so long searching, and hitherto in vain. Dr. Bernard Davis considered that " the form of the Neanderthal skull was the result of a *synoptasis ;* " * and as this then newly-coined word technically means " ossification of the sutures," being derived from the Greek *sun-ousia*, which the lexicon describes as " a meeting of friends," we may conclude that the skull acquired its ape-like shape from its converse with such a large family party as were gathered in the scientific circle at Bonn.

Suddenly a voice was heard issuing from the interior of the skull, which recalled to mind a tradition current in medieval times respecting the skull of a

---

* See Dr. Davis' Essay on the subject, in the first volume of the *Anthropological Review.*

Christian martyr found in the Roman catacombs, which was said to have rewarded its discoverer by informing him of its name, age, and some interesting antecedents, the truth of which was confirmed by a learned Canonist explaining that "it was without doubt *an angel which did speak in the skull.*"*

As soon as the vast assembly had sufficiently expressed their opinions on the object before them, and had subsided into that happy state of silence which betokens the height of expectation, the voice from the skull delivered the following address:—

SPEECH OF THE NEANDERTHAL SKULL.

Gentlemen, and with your permission I will add, dear Relatives and Friends, I might begin my address with the usual formula, "Unaccustomed as I am to public speaking," for many centuries have rolled by since I last addressed such a learned assembly, and my old jaws have

---

* Alphonsus Mendoza, *Controv. Theol.* Quæst. vi. Scholiast, § 5.

grown rusty for want of practice in the art of elocution. I will, however, try to do my best, while trusting to your kind indulgence for the mistakes I may commit on the present occasion.

During my long retirement I have witnessed with much satisfaction the wonderful advance of Science in these latter days, in its various branches, more especially in that which relates to the human race, as the Greek philosopher Epicurus justly remarked—

"*We are a sufficient theme for contemplation, the one for the other.*"

And one of your own poets sings in the same strain, when he says—

"*Know thou thyself, presume not man to scan,*
The proper study of mankind is MAN."

It is truer now than it was two centuries ago, when the erratic Lord Chancellor Brougham gave utterance to his memorable saying, "The schoolmaster is abroad;" and I am sanguine enough to believe that his travels have not yet come to an end.

It has been thought by some high authorities that in consequence of the express-train system of education in the present day, many novel theories are broached solely for the purpose of criticism, then laid aside and forgotten as if they had never existed. I am not prepared to say whether this is correct or not, but it may be safely assumed that many such theories pass through the three stages of startling announcement, hasty acceptance, and silent retraction; since it must be confessed that if your Professors of Science are often highly original in their speculative theories, they are often very loose in attempting to verify them. To mention a case in point. One of the most distinguished scientists of the 19th century, Professor Tyndall, has truly observed that "without *verification*, a theoretic conception is a mere figment of the intellect."* Although this remark is made " On Prayer as a Form of Physical Energy," it has been applied with no little

* See Tyndall's *Fragments of Science*, p. 469.

force to the doctrine of EVOLUTION, which will be the chief subject of my address to night. Dr. Elam has pointed this out in the form of a syllogism. Without *verification* a theoretic conception is a mere figment of the intellect. The theory of Organic Evolution is an unverified theoretic conception. Therefore *Organic Evolution* is *a mere figment of the Intellect.**

This doctrine is of so powerful a nature, that according to some of its advocates inorganic dead matter will evolve organic life—the fortuitous concourse of atoms has created the universe; the primeval fungus and the ascidian tadpole have alike been credited with the power of gradually developing themselves into a being, which your Bible teaches was originally created "after the image and likeness of God." On this point, however, your learned doctors greatly differ among themselves. Professor OWEN, probably the first authority among Naturalists of the 19th century, declared that "observa-

* *Contemporary Review* for 1880.

tion of the actual change of any one species into another *has not yet been found ;*" while Professor Haeckel, on the other hand, intrepidly maintained that the transition from invertebrates to vertebrates was clearly seen in that interesting little animal the *sand-eel.* And Professor Huxley confidently taught the curious dogma of lobsters and sheep being " transubstantiated into man."*

As the Transmutation system of your modern scientists bears a strong family resemblance to the Transmigration theory of the ancients, and as this bears upon the doctrine of Evolution and the Origin of Man, and was so keenly discussed in the 19th century, I propose to notice the ideas which have been put forth by eminent men on these points, both ancient and modern, in due chronological order.

The earliest authority on this subject is the famous philosopher PYTHAGORAS, who flourished in the 6th century B.C., and you are indebted to your most celebrated

* Huxley's *Lay Sermons,* p. 146.

dramatist, the "immortal" Shakespeare,[*] for informing you what the great Grecian thought on this subject. In one of his *comedies* he represents one of his characters asking the following question—

"*Clown.*—What was the opinion of Pythagoras concerning wild fowl?

"*Malvolio.*—That the soul of our great grand-dam might haply inhabit a bird.

"*Clown.*—What thinkest thou of this opinion?

"*Malvolio.*—I think nobly of the soul, and in no wise receive his opinion." [†]

Let me remind you that Shakespeare's own opinion respecting the origin of man seems rather to coincide with that of your distinguished Naturalist, Mr. Darwin, whose philosophy I propose to consider at length, rather than with that of Pythagoras, for he describes your simian ancestor in these words :—

---

[*] It is far too large a question to consider here, but very grave doubts have been raised, chiefly by the American critics, as to the real authorship of Shakespeare."

[†] *Twelfth Night; or What you Will.* Act iv., sc. 2, l. 53.

"But man, proud man,
Drest in a little brief authority,
Most ignorant of what he's most assured,
His glassy essence, *like an angry ape*,
Plays such fantastic tricks before high heaven
As make the angels weep : who, with our spleens,
Would all themselves laugh mortal." *

Shakespeare's theory of the proud Englishman's resemblance to "an angry *ape*," has been supplemented by Voltaire's definition of a Frenchman being composed of "half tiger and half monkey," and confirmed by the great German historian Niebuhr, who when speaking of the Italians says their " life is little more than that of an *ape* endowed with speech."

The next in chronological order would be the "divine" Plato, as he has been termed by his ardent admirers, and I only give the precedence to Aristotle, who was born 40 years later than Plato, because his testimony is so brief, but pointed. In his work entitled *De Gente Animalium*, he gives this alternative view of man's origin. "Supposing," he says, " both man and

---

* *Measure for Measure*, act ii., scene 2, l. 120.

animals to have sprung from earth, they must have done so in one of two ways— either they crawled out as *worms*, or they came out as *eggs*."

PLATO, the most celebrated of all the Grecian philosophers, represents Socrates, the wisest of the wise, as advocating the Transmutation theory to its fullest extent, by supposing that the wicked, after their penal wanderings of 10,000 years in the world of spirits, would again return to earth, and be " turned into asses and brutes of that kind; " while the souls of the good would " again migrate into a corresponding peaceable kind of animal, such as bees or wasps, or ants, or even into the same species again, and from these become *moderate men*." *

But it is in another work where Plato's talent shines out so brightly, in the description which he gives in his *Banquet*, or *Treatise on Love*, of the origin of the human race, and which is deserving of

---

* Plato's *Phædo*, § 70. Herodotus only allows 3000 years as the limit of the Transmigration period.

your most attentive consideration. He gives Aristophanes the credit of this original suggestion, but we may suppose without doubt that it is his own transcendental idea; which he explains as follows:—

Although men appear to be insensible to the power of Love, since they build no altars in its honour, as all priests ever will do in honour of those whom they worship, I will endeavour to explain its power in order that you may teach others. But you must first learn the nature of man, and what sufferings it has undergone. For *our nature of old was not what it is now*. Originally there was no such thing known as difference of sex. Every one was male and female alike, perfect in form, faculties and spirit. The exact shape of this being was a round ball of flesh, with four hands and four legs, with two faces upon a circular neck alike in every way, one head with four ears, and only one brain—not unlike one of your early progenitors, according to the high authority of Darwin, who teaches that the primeval ancestor of all the vertebratæ was "an aquatic animal, with the two sexes united in the same individual." *

During the period of undivided sexes, this creature was a pattern of strength and speed. He could fell an ox as easily as Hercules; and when he wished to take a gallop, he had only to thrust out his four legs and four arms, and roll along the road like a wheel which had lost its tire. But these beings, which in reality were three in one, the male, the female, and the two combined, were the offspring of various parts of the solar system. The male kind was the produce of the *sun*, the female of the *earth*, and that which partook of the other two of the *moon*. Hence these creatures, proud of their shape and power, attempted to scale the heavens. Jupiter, unwilling to destroy the whole race as he had done to the giants, hit upon a plan by which man might still exist, though greatly shorn

---

* *Descent of Man,* i. 206; ii. 389.

of his strength. So the great Jove proceeded to cut these creatures into two parts, as you cut oranges when about to eat them.

Great was the consternation at this loss of power, the agony of cutting two sides asunder being intense. For man thus shorn of his rotundity could no longer wrestle with the lion, nor outstrip the deer. Each part of the divided creature was compelled now to stand upon two legs—a feat of much skill, the art of which he was slow to learn and swift to lose. Every step he attempted to take only showed him his loss of original power; and that the gods had laid upon him a burden too heavy to bear.

And this was not the worst. Besides having to pass his life in trying to stand on two legs, man found to his sorrow that he was parted from his better half. When the rebel rotundities were cleft in twain, the two halves were scattered in different parts of the world. Each wounded part sought its fellow, but the gods took care that much of the search should be made in vain. This act of celestial vengeance broke down man's spirit entirely. Alone in the cold world, and perched up in the air on two legs only, what could he do in the midst of his grief? Once indeed he felt inclined to rebel, but Jupiter quickly let him know that if he did not keep quiet, he should be split once more from the crown downwards, so that in future he would have to stand on one leg alone.

Man listened to this threat in an agony of fear, and submitted without any further murmuring. All that was left to him of his former bliss was a yearning hope of one day finding his own better half. Thus each man became a searcher, though only a few were fortunate enough to find their mates. Most had to seek for them long, and myriads never found them at all. When any one was fortunate enough to fall in with his own "better half," a true marriage of the spirit took place. To this longing desire of the cleft

C

parts for union has been given the name of
LOVE.   And so, adds the sage, by way of
moral, "let us take care not to offend the
gods, lest we be cleft in twain, and have to
go about with noses slit down, and have to
stand for the future on one leg alone!"*

One of your modern scientists, in his
description of the Egyptian cosmogony,
shows that it did not materially differ from
the dual principle mentioned by Plato: as
he defines it on this wise—"When the
first chaotic mass had been produced in
the form of an egg by a self-dependent and
eternal Being, it required the mysterious
functions of this *masculo-feminine* demiurgos
to reduce the component elements into
organised forms"—adding, with malicious
gravity, "Although it is scarcely possible to
recall to mind this conceit without smiling,
it does not seem to differ essentially in principle
from some cosmological notions of men of
great genius and science in modern
Europe." †

---

* Plato's *Banquet*, §§ 16—19.
† Sir Charles Lyell's *Principles of Geology*, ch. ii.

Besides this mundane egg theory of Egyptian cosmogony, that of Transmutation was resuscitated in the 19th century by some of your scientists as the best mode of explaining the origin of the human race. Perhaps the earliest propounder of this theory was the Latin poet OVID,* as he describes in his *Metamorphosis* the many changes which a sacred hierophant represents himself to have undergone before becoming one of the human race—" I have been a blue salmon, a dog, a stag, a roebuck on the mountains, a stock of a tree, a spade, an axe in the head, a pin in a forceps for a year and a half, a cock variegated with white, a horse, a buck of yellow hue in the act of feeding. I have been a grain vegetating on a hill. I was received by a hen with red fangs, and remained nine nights an infant inside her. I have been in Hades; I have died; I have revived; and conspicuous with my ivy branch, I have been a leader, and by my bounty I became *poor*."

* See Appendix A.

c 2

GUATAMA BUDDHA, the founder of the Buddhist religion, upheld very strongly this Transmutation theory; and his followers in Japan pay such respect unto their ancestors of the Simian tribe, that apes and monkeys are visibly worshipped in their pagodas, in the same way that Roman Catholics adore the images and pictures of their dead saints. And so careful are they of the parental stock in that happy land, that hospitals are generously provided for the sick and poor apes,* just as in Protestant England they are established for those of your own sick and poor who need them so much; so that you may in course of time hear of an annual hospital sermon in Japan for the sick monkeys, just as you have one in London in the present day. In the Archives of the Propaganda at Rome there exists a letter addressed in 1742 by Mi-Vang, the Grand Lama of Thibet, to Pope Benedict XIV., in which he speaks of the happiness enjoyed by the

---

* Dr. Hurd's *Religious Rites and Ceremonies of All Nations*, p. 105.

Buddhists through their firm belief in the doctrine of *Metempsychosis* on "the Transmutation theory," which the founder of the Buddhist religion underwent twenty-two times before attaining the dignity of man, exactly the same number as Professor Hæckel has given to the prehistoric progenitors of the human race. Thus Guatama Buddha was evolved from these various animals, until he finally appeared in all the dignity of an Indian prince. 1. Originally he was hid in the spirit of a tree. 2. Then he became a fish. 3. Then he evolved into a frog. 4. The bird *Housa*. 5. A jungle fowl. 6. A water fowl. 7. Snipe. 8. Woodpecker. 9. A cock. 10. Crow. 11. Golden eagle. 12. Then he passed from the produce of an egg into the mammalia kind—as a pig. 13. Then a rat. 14. Dog. 15. Hare. 16. Bull. 17. Horse. 18. Deer. 19. Lion. 20. Elephant. 21. Jackall. 22. Ape. Finally he appeared in the world under these seven disguises, as—1. A slave. 2. A gambler. 3. A thief. 4. A scientist. 5. A merchant. 6. A priest.

7. Until finally he arrived at the dignity of an Indian king.*

Six centuries after the time of Ovid, the Transmutation theory was firmly held by your British ancestors. TALIESSEN, the most distinguished of the Welsh bards, who became a Christian before he died, represented himself as having been successively "a serpent, a wild ass, a brick and a crane," until he settled down in life as a quiet country squire, and a very determined opponent to the rising claims of the Popes of Rome.

Similar views of the Transmutation theory appear to have prevailed in the Emerald Isle, as it had done in Wales. One of your famous chroniclers, quaint old GIRALDUS CAMBRIENSIS, of the 12th century, represents the aborigines of Ireland as having all been drowned by the Noachian Flood, save one, Titan, who was saved by having been transmuted into a *salmon*, from whom all the post-diluvian inhabitants of the island are said to have been descended. Hence a native

---

* *Manual of Buddhism, p.* 100.

tradition current amongst the Irish at that time, that "the souls of them that were drowned at the Flood were supposed to be enchanted in the bodies of the seals, which once swarmed upon the Western Coast of Ireland, undergoing *water purgatory*"! HUMBOLT mentions a somewhat similar tradition once current amongst the Aztecs of Mexico. "Before the great Flood, the country of Anahuac was inhabited by giants. All those who did not perish were *transformed into fishes*, except seven, who fled into a cavern."*

Should you wish to have the opinion of a modern authority of the very highest class on the doctrine of Transmutation, I would quote that of the celebrated AGASSIZ in proof of what I must frankly confess is the case, that the weight of all rational argument is quite fatal to it—as he says, "The conviction which draws me irresistibly is, that the combination of animals on this continent where the faunæ are so characteristic and so distinct from all

* Humbolt's *Researches.* &c., vol. i., p. 96.

others, will give me the means of showing
that the *Transmutation theory is wholly
without foundation in fact.*"*

Five centuries after Giraldus, a French
herbalist named GERARD, traced the origin
of the *Pentalasmus antefera,* or " five-plated
goose bearer," to the *Barnacle leucopsis,* or
" bernicle goose," which, he says, " grows
on one of your British isles off the coast of
Lancashire," and comes from what is
familiarly known as *" the ship barnacle."*
As the ancient Grecians used to declare of
the lovely Venus Aphrodite, Gerard contended that *the spume* exuding from pieces
of rotten timber cast upon the isle by
shipwracke *breedeth muskles,* and when the
muskles is perfectly formed the shell gapeth
open, and the first thing that appeareth is
a bit of *string*; next come *the legs of a bird*
hanging out, which in short cometh to
full maturitie and falleth into the sea,
where it gathereth feathers, and groweth
into a *fowle.*"

Gerard's theory of the tribe of birds in

---

* Agassiz's *Travels in Brazil,* p. 33.

general, and the bernicle goose in particular, being descended from " rotten
timber," is not original. It was a medieval
fable adopted by Saxo Grammaticus and
Giraldus in the dark ages, as well as by
the learned Joseph Scaliger and Bishop
Leslie in more modern days. Giraldus
especially explains how the " barnacles
grew from timber, being bred in a very
unaccountable and curious manner by the
juices of the wood in the sea water;"
adding, that as " no eggs are laid by these
birds after pairing, as is the case with birds
in general, bishops and religious men in
Ireland make no scruple of eating these
birds on fasting days as not being *flesh*,
because they are not born of flesh."* This
will remind you of Professor HUXLEY'S
teaching concerning the danger of supping
on lobsters, for then, he says, the matter of
life of the crustacean would undergo the
same (he had previously been speaking of
sheep being transubstantiated into man) won-

---

* *Topography of Ireland*, by Giraldus Cambriensis,
Dist. i., ch. xi.

derful metamorphosis into humanity."*   I
am inclined to think that your noted lay
preacher has been here rather guilty of a
plagiarism, as Aquileius of old tells you in
his book of the *Golden Ass*, that on one
occasion, when drinking a certain potion,
he had been transubstantiated into *an ass*,
while at the same time he retained his
human mind.   And so Giraldus, whom I
have before quoted, declares that he had
seen " persons who by magical arts turned
any substance about them into *fat pigs*, as
they appeared, though always of a red
colour, and sold them in the markets."†

A countryman of Gerard's, BENOIT DE
MAILLET, Consul - General of France in
Egypt, during the reign of Louis XIV., in
his work *Telliamed*, improves upon Gerard's
theory of evolving the bernacle goose from
rotten timber, as he argues that the whole
tribe of birds once existed as *marine animals*,
which on being thrown ashore by the waves
had got feathers by accident, and that

---

* Huxley's *Lay Sermons*, p. 146.
† *Topography of Ireland*, Dist. ii., ch. xix.

mankind were the descendants of a tribe of sea monsters, who, on getting tired of their proper element, crawled up the beach one fine morning, and taking a fancy to the land, either forgot or felt a disinclination to return. From these terrestrioaquatic animals, Maillet considers the human race to have sprung.

Before Maillet had evolved this brilliant idea respecting the origin of your race, we meet with the germ of that theory which took such firm hold of many of your *savans*, though not of the first class, in the 19th century, viz., that monkeys were the ancestors of mankind. HENRY MOORE, whose *Conjectura Cabbalistica* was published A.D. 1662, somewhat severely condemns this theory by observing— "Of a truth vile epicurism and sensuality will make the soul of man so degenerate and blind, that he will not only be content to slide into brutish immorality, but please himself in this very opinion that *he is a real brute already, an ape* or *a baboon*, and that the best of men are

no better, save that civilization and
industrious education have made them
appear in a more refined shape, and long-
inculcated precepts have been mistaken
for cognate principles of honesty and
natural knowledge."

The theory of your ape descent was
more confidently set forth in the
following century by the celebrated
Scotch judge, James Burnett, more familiarly known by his title of LORD
MONBODDO, who boldly traced your
pedigree from monkeys, and affirmed that
in some countries men had tails like other
beasts. Your great lexicographer, Dr.
JOHNSON, was thought—vainly, as time has
proved—to have put down his foot on
the theory by observing, " Of a standing
fact, sir, there ought to be no controversy;
if there are men with tails, they hide them,
but Monboddo is as jealous of his tail as a
squirrel."* One of your most distinguished
professors of the 19th century, a really
learned man apart from his being called a

---

* Boswell's *Life of Johnson*, iv. 73.

professor, the celebrated MAX MULLER, somewhat sarcastically observes on the same subject—"Lord Monboddo had just finished his great work in which he derives all mankind *from a couple of asses*, and the dialects of the world from a language originally framed by some Egyptian gods." *

Shortly after Lord Monboddo had propounded his theory of man's descent from a monkey, the philosophic LAMARCK endeavoured to put the whole subject of Development or Evolution into scientific ship-shape by reasoning thus—"You see in Nature," he said, "a gradation of organized beings, therefore we must admit a series of successive changes by which animals of one class can raise themselves to another. For example, a bird compelled by necessity to seek for water, either swims or passes through places of little depth, and its descendants do the same. During the course of many generations, the efforts which it made to extend its claws, would

---

* See Appendix B.

cause the formation of a membrane, and it would thus become to all intents a *water bird;* or it might extend its feet still more by passing through still deeper waters, and gradually its legs would become as long as those of a crane or flamingo. These two actions, combined with fresh desires aud a natural tendency to satisfy them, have united *to form man from a monkey.* A species of these animals, probably that of the *orang-outang,* though of this all remembrance has been lost (no specimen of the missing link having yet been found), began to climb trees, and to seize them with its *hinder* hands as well as with those *before.* After having thus walked on the ground for many generations, the hinder limbs became formed in a manner suitable to their habits, and feet appeared, by which means these animals were enabled to walk upright. They had no need of their paws for the purpose of gathering fruit or fighting; they were able to employ their fore-feet which were turned into hands, and hence by degrees

the snout became shortened, and therefore
more vertical......When the orang-outang
is compelled to take to flight from very
pressing danger, he immediately falls
down on all fours, proving that such must
have been the primitive condition of the
animal; and thus children, who have large
heads and prominent stomachs, can hardly
walk at two years old, and their frequent
tumbles indicate the natural tendency to
resume the quadrupal state." *

In one of the ballads of the 19th
century, which is supposed to point
directly to the Evolution doctrine of Mr.
Darwin, but which in reality belongs
to Lamarck, as the original propounder
of the view so charmingly advocated by
his disciple, who has by his talent made
the theory popular, Lamarck's idea of the
short-legged shore bird gradually developing itself into the long-legged stork;
or the short-necked deer, by continually
stretching in order to graze on the top-
most branches, in time evolved itself into

* See Appendix C.

a giraffe—is thus faithfully expressed in the following lines:—

"Have you heard this strange theory the doctors
      among,
  That all living things from *a monad* have sprung?
  This thing has been said, and now shall be sung ...
  A very tall pig with a very long nose,
  Sent down a proboscis quite close to his toes,
  And then by the name of an *elephant* goes.
  A deer with a neck which was longer by half
  Than most of his family—please not to laugh—
  By stretching and stretching becomes a giraffe.
  An ape with a pliable thumb and big brain,
  When the gift of the gab he had managed to gain,
  As a lord of creation established his reign," &c.

Lamarck's theory may remind you of an anecdote respecting a British officer in India, who when trying to convince a native of the value of converting *iron into steel*, received this sage reply—"What! would have me then believe that if I put an *ass* into a furnace it will come forth a *horse?*" Such a sensible reply is only to be paralleled by the overflowing wit of the Irish lad, when he exclaimed in reply to his English master, who had been tormenting him with some stupid questions,

"Sure, your honour, would I be a horse if I were born in a stable?"

The force of the Evolution theory has been well exemplified in the case of another wit from the Emerald Isle, who on the occasion of his being tried for stealing *a gun* manfully defended himself, and with heart-searching eloquence, so characteristic of his native land, endeavoured to convince the judge and the jury that he had been the rightful owner of the gun, which was found in his possession, *from the time it had been a very little pistol!* And when he found that his pleading was of no avail, but that the jury unhesitatingly found him guilty from the strong evidence adduced against him, he burst forth with the following peroration:—

"An' myself guilty is it, avick? An' I the owner of the *shooting animal, the poor baaste?* from whin 'twere a gorsoon of a pistol! No, goodwill to ye, jhoodge an' jhoory! For sure there's small acquintance wid the langidges, or wid Misther Euclid's *ailments* an' *logicals*, or, *agra*, wid Misther

Dhurwin's Ivillootions! *Musha*, no philo-
maths them spalpeens! Our hedge-schul-
masther 'd tak' the consate out on 'm all
in no time! No comparishment between
'm! Och! an' 'tis a bad job intirely! An'
the misfortunate crathur is myself, avour-
neen! Och! Katty, beloved of my heart!
an' how will ye dig the phaties for thim
sivin childer, an' anither, one at laaste!
sune to foller.   Och! Katty, pulse of my
life! Och! Och! Och! Och!" *

Contemporary with Lamarck flourished
Dr. ERASMUS DARWIN, grandfather of his
more distinguished namesake, who in his
Botanic Garden mentions the Evolution
theory as conceived by a philosophic
friend, who declared that the first insects
were the anthers or stigmas of flowers,
which had somehow released themselves
from the parent plant; and that other
insects gradually evolved themselves from
them, some acquiring wings, others fins,
and others claws, from their efforts to

* *Divine Revelation, or Pseudo-Science ?* An Essay;
by R. G. S. Browne, B.D.; pp. 62, 63.

procure food, or to protect themselves from injury.

But inasmuch as this theory has been so brilliantly stated by the celebrated Mr. Canning, author of the *Anti-Jacobin*, let me remind you of his clever conception of the origin of all things in general, and the doctrine of evolution in particular. " We may conceive," argued Mr. CANNING, " the whole of our present universe to have been originally concentrated in a single point, we may conceive this primeval point, or *punctum saliens* of the universe, *evolving itself* by its own energies, to have moved forward in a right line *ad infinitum* until it grew tired ; after which the right line which it had generated would begin to put itself in motion in a lateral direction, describing an area of infinite extent. This area, *as it became conscious of its own existence*, would begin to ascend according as its specific gravity would determine it, forming an immense solid space filled with vacuum, and capable of containing the present universe. Space being thus obtained, and presenting a suitable *nidus*, or receptacle for the accumulation of chaotic matter, an immense deposit of it would be gradually accumulated, after which the filament of fire being produced in the chaotic mass by an idiosyncrasy, or self-formed habit analogous to fermentation, explosions would take place, suns would be shot from the central chaos, planets from suns, and satellites from planets. In this state of things the filament of organization would begin to exert itself in those independent masses which in proportion to their bulk would expose the greatest surface to light and heat. This filament, after an infinite series of ages, would begin to ramify, and its oviparous offspring would diversify their former habits, so as to accommodate themselves to their various *incunabula* which nature had prepared for them. Upon this view of things, it seems highly probable that the first efforts of nature terminated in the production of *vegetables*, and that these being abandoned *to their own energies* by degrees, detached themselves from the surface of the earth, and supplied themselves with wings and feet according as their different propensities determined them in favour of aerial or terrestrial existence. Others, by an inherent disposition to society and civilization, and by a stronger effort of volition, would *become men*. These in time would restrict themselves to the use of their hind feet, and *their tails* would gradually rub off by sitting in their caves or huts as they arrived at a domesticated state. They would then *invent language* and the use of fire. In the meanwhile the *fuci* and *algæ* would transform themselves into fish, and would gradually populate all the submarine portion of the globe."

This fine theory of insects having evolved themselves from flowers, as suggested by Dr. Darwin the elder, combined with the very original idea of the way by which the first men got rid of their ancestral tails, as propounded by one of the three great statesmen of the 19th century, is the earliest and most lucid statement of the

dogma of evolution which has yet appeared :
but whether it will stand the test of a
critical examination remains to be seen.
About the same time that Mr. Canning had
evolved his brilliant idea from his inner
consciousness, Professor OKEN, of Zurich,
plunged deeper into the recesses of the new
philosophy, and determining to trace the
origin of man further back than to vegetables, or even the primeval point, took one
step more backwards, and announced as his
peculiar discovery that man's earliest ancestor was in reality NOTHING ! His opinion
is expressed in the following way :—

"The highest mathematical idea is that
ZERO $=$ O.   Zero is itself *nothing*.   Mathe-
matics are based upon *nothing*, and
consequently arise out of *nothing*.   The
Eternal is *the nothing of Nature*.   There
exists *nothing but nothing;* nothing but the
Eternal.   Man is God wholly manifested.
God has become man.   Zero has become
+.   For God to become real, He must
appear under the form of the sphere; God
is a rotating globe.   The world is God

rotating. Every thing that is, is immaterial. Self-consciousness is a living ellipse.

" Physico-philosophy has to portray the first period of the world's development *out of nothing;* how the elements and heavenly bodies originated by self-evolution into higher and manifold forms, then separated into minerals, became finally organic, and in man attained to self-consciousness. No organism has been created of larger size than an *infusorial point.* Whatever is larger has not been created, but developed. *Man has not been created, but developed.* As the human body has been formed by the extreme separation of the mucous mass, so must the human mind be a separation, *a memberment of infusorial sensation !*"

Oken's idea of the origin of all things may be traced up to MOSCHUS the Egyptian, but I am not quite sure whether he did not steal it from the Buddhist philosophy; which is tersely expressed in the aphorism—

" *Man's mind is divine, but most divine when nearest nothing.*"

But this has been barbarously parodied by one of your own poets, in his famous apostrophe of Oken's round O—

"When naught is everything, and everything is naught."

Speaking, however, with the utmost frankness, as I am sure all honest men would wish me to do, I am sorry to say one of your great classical writers of the 19th century has surpassed all the above-mentioned authorities, whether it be Oken, Lucretius, Moschus, or the Buddhist philosopher, who can only go so far as " nothing," in endeavouring to trace the origin of man to the infusorial point, or to *nothing;* for De Quincey goes one step beyond, even to that *terra incognita* " less than nothing." And this he does in a very heart-rending, sarcastic way, which I hope will not disturb the feelings of any of the Professorial Fellows of the Royal Society whom I have the honour to see before me.

A Frenchman named Piron, the cynical author of *La Métromanie*, having written the following epitaph on himself—

Ce git Piron ; qui ne fuit rien ;
Pas même académicien—

De Quincey rendered it in English thus—

"Here lies Piron ; who was—*nothing ;*
Or, if *that* could be, was less ;
How! Nothing? Yes, nothing ;
Not so much as F.R.S. ! "—

These cabbalistic letters so much valued, having the double meaning of *Fellow of the Royal Society*, and also (oh! tell it not in Gath) of *Fellow Remarkably Stupid !*

Another of your famous poets, though belonging to the Emerald Isle, Tom Moore, adopting the theory of the Jewish Rabbins, that the account in the Book of Genesis of Eve, the first woman, having been taken from the *rib* of Adam is a misrendering, and that the word should have been "*tail*" instead, thus happily expresses himself on the subject—

"They tell us that woman was made of a *rib*,
　Just picked from a corner so snug in the side ;
But the Rabbins declare that this is a fib,
　And 'twas not so at all that the sex was supplied.

For old Adam was fashioned the first of his kind,
  With a tail like a monkey, full yard and a span;
And when Nature cut off this appendage behind,
  Why—then woman was made of *the tail of the man !*"

More than a quarter of a century elapsed after Moore had thus explained the teaching of the Jewish Rabbins respecting the Origin of Man, when the anonymous author of a work entitled *Vestiges of the Natural History of Creation*, evolved a scheme of human geology showing that Adam's immediate ancestor was a *chimpanzee*, and his remote ancestor a *maggot!* He grounded his conclusion upon these two points—1st, That the basis of all vegetable and animal substance consists of nucleated cells, *i.e.*, cells having "granules" within them. 2dly, That the organization of man gradually passes through conditions resembling a *worm*, a fish, a reptile, a bird, and the lower *mammalia*, before it attains its maturity in man.

But this theory of man's descent from worms was one of the many plagiarisms of the learned professors of the 19th century. I have already reminded you that it is one of the alternative theories of Aristotle; and it was also held by the savage philosophers of Tahiti, who seem to be of the same opinion; as they declare that the origin of your race may be traced to a heap of vegetables in the act of rotting, which gave rise to a number of *worms*, and out of these said worms men and women were at length evolved!

Having already given you the opinion of the celebrated Mr. Canning on the origin of man, I will add, in conclusion, before taking up the teaching of Professor Darwin, that of another Prime Minister, Mr. Disraeli, or as known in his later years by the title of Lord Beaconsfield. Before publishing a work of fiction called *Tancred, or the New Crusade*, he had declared it was a question whether men had originally been *apes* or *angels;* but in *Tancred* he states the subject with more scientific precision.

"You must read the *Revelation of Chaos*, which I will lend you," says a blue-

stocking lady to the hero; "every thing
is there explained scientifically by geology and astronomy. It shows you exactly how a star is formed; nothing can
be so pretty! A cluster of vapour, the
cream of the milky way, a sort of celestial
cheese churned into light. But what is
most interesting is the way in which man
has been developed. You know all is
development. The principle is perpetually
going on. First there was nothing; then
there was something; then I forget the
next. I think there were shells, then
fishes; then we came at last. The next
change there will be something very
superior to us, something with wings.
Ah! that's it; we were fishes, and we shall
be crows. We had fins; we may have
wings."

Such was the expression of a distinguished politician on the much disputed
questions of the 19th century—viz., the
origin of men and things, and the
theory of AGNOSTIC EVOLUTION. And
inasmuch as these doctrines by universal

consent are inseparably connected with the name of one of your most illustrious Scientists, I propose to devote the next portion of my address to a careful consideration of the various theories enunciated by the renowned CHARLES DARWIN; and in order to avoid the possibility of misrepresenting his views, I will first quote his *ipsissima verba*, and then proceed to comment on the doctrine which the natural meaning of his words appears to teach.

PROFESSOR DARWIN.

I now come to consider the claims of a very distinguished Naturalist, the famous Charles Darwin, to rank as the first philosopher of the 19th century, and whom Professor Huxley has placed on a par with the immortal Newton, and has termed him the greatest *savant* evolved from an ape next to Aristotle. Although we naturally smile at such a rhapsodical simile, I gladly avow my respect for the great Naturalist, as he was both a learned and a modest

man, with a tender feeling towards those
who dissented from his views, which cannot be said with truth of many of his disciples, who endeavour to trade on his
honoured name. And in order that I may
do him full justice, I propose to quote some
extracts from his chief works before proceeding to comment on his opinions, and
to show you clearly wherein their error
lays.

Under the high-sounding names of
Natural Selection—Development—Evolution—Transmutation — Pangenesis—Biogenesis—Abiogenesis—Agamogenesis—*
Osmosis—Protoplasm—Physical Basis of
Life, and others of a still wilder nomen-
clature, which appear to have been invented, as Curran humorously said of the
Round Towers in Ireland, more for the
purpose " of puzzling posterity" than any
thing else, some of your Scientists have
succeeded in bewitching a large number
of the unlearned world in general, together

* See Appendix D.

with a few of those who may be termed real *savans* in particular.

Under the double terms of Natural Selection and Evolution, Mr. Charles Darwin, grandson of Dr. Erasmus Darwin, author of the *Botanic Garden,* has persuaded himself, and has succeeded in persuading many others to believe, that the human race has primarily descended from the larvæ of an ascidian tadpole, and finally from an old-world monkey.

His early opinion of the Transmutation theory is thus charmingly explained. In his *Origin of Species* he accounts for various changes of one species of quadrupeds, and especially for the enormous head of the *cetacea,* in the following instructive manner :—" I will give two or three instances of diversified and changed habits in the individuals of the same species. When either case occurs, it would be easy for *Natural Selection* to fit the animal by some modification of its structure for its changed habits. . . . Let the organization of a dog be *slightly plastic ;* let the number of rabbits decrease and the number of hares increase, the dog would be driven to catch more hares, the less fleet ones would be rigidly destroyed. I see no reason to doubt that those causes in thousands of generations would produce a marked effect. . . . In North America, the black bear was seen by Hearne swimming for hours with a widely-open mouth ; thus catching *almost like a whale* insects in the water. *I see no difficulty* in a race of bears being rendered by *Natural Selection* more and more aquatic in their structure and habits, with larger and larger mouths, till a creature was produced *as monstrous as a whale.*"*

For some unexplained reason this instructive specimen of the Transmutation theory, by which Natural Selection evolves a whale from a black bear, was omitted after the first edition, possibly because a deeper study of the subject increased rather than lessened Mr. Darwin's " difficulties." Though in the case of pigs being

---

* Darwin's *Origin of Species*, p. 184.

transmuted into elephants by the power of Natural Selection he still continues to believe, observing in the same work that "pigs have often been born with a sort of proboscis" (p. 89).

It must not, however, be supposed for a moment that Darwin entertained Materialistic or Atheistic notions like most of his disciples, for he distinctly says—"I believe that animals have descended from at most only four or five progenitors, and plants from an equal or lesser number. Analogy would lead me one step further, viz., to the belief that all animals and plants have descended from some prototype. But analogy may be a deceitful guide. Nevertheless, all living things have much in common. Therefore I should infer from analogy that *probably* all the organic beings which have ever lived on this earth have descended *from some one primordial form*, into which life was first breathed by the Creator."*

---

* Darwin's *Origin of Species*, p. 484.

E

In reply to the very serious objection to the Transmutation theory, such as bears becoming whales in course of time, or pigs growing into elephants, that no single case of one species being evolved from another having come within the observation ' of man, Mr. Darwin replies that though " Geology does not reveal any such finely graduated organic chain—and this perhaps is the most obvious and gravest objection which can be urged against my theory— the explanation lies, as I believe, in *the extreme imperfection of the geological record. If my theory be true*, it is indisputable that before the lowest Silurian stratum was deposited, long periods elapsed, as long as, or perhaps far longer than, the whole interval from the Silurian age to the present day." One period he estimates to a nicety, as follows : "I should infer that the denudation of the weald (alone) must have required 306,662,400 years, or say three hundred millions."

Darwin cautiously guards himself on this, as on many other occasions, by that

powerful protector, an "If." "If my theory
be true," that every vestige of this long
geological period, which according to his
estimate may have included some *millions
of years*, has entirely disappeared, what
becomes of the argument so frequently
advanced by the Atheistic school that
matter is indestructible, and that these
lengthy æons, during which, as Darwin
says, "these vast unknown periods of time
the earth swarmed with living creatures,"
have not left a sign of their material substance behind them. If one half of the
geological formations known to us, and
which is computed to consist of upwards of
40 statute miles in thickness, has produced
such a rich harvest of fossil fauna and flora
to prove that they once existed as living
things and creatures on the then surface
of the earth, why has the other half,
according to the Darwinian philosophy,
so entirely disappeared .as to leave no
single trace of its entity? Surely you
must see that in place of there being
any imperfection or non-existence of

the geological record, the imperfection is rather in Mr. Darwin's reasoning powers.

In support of his principle of Nature working by *Natural Selection*, Darwin acknowledges that "*if* it could be demonstrated that any complete organ existed which could not possibly have been formed by numerous successive slight modifications, *my theory would absolutely break down.*" *

The believer in the teleological argument, that the Supreme Creator worked by design, when He pronounced all things "very good," naturally thinks of such an object as "the eye," in contradiction of this speculative theory; but Darwin has anticipated him by candidly owning the weakness of his own argument. "To suppose that the eye with all its inimitable contrivances for adjusting the focus to different distances, for admitting different amounts of light, and for the correction of

---

* *Origin of Species*, p. 189.

spherical and chromatic aberration, could have been formed by *Natural Selection,* seems, I freely confess, *absurd in the highest possible degree.*" *

I suppose most persons possessed with the average amount of common sense will agree with him. Nevertheless, there are infidels bold enough to declare that this complicated and wonderful organ, the eye, which gives evidence of an Almighty designer more than any thing else in creation, so far from this, proves to be a very poor specimen of workmanship in their estimation. The late Professor W. K. Clifford, in an address to the British Association of 1872, on *Aims and Instruments of Scientific Thought,* while pointedly denying that "every thing has a cause or a purpose," quotes the authority of Helmholtz, a German physiologist, on the formation "of the eye," as he said, "If an optician sent me that as an instrument, I should send it back to him with grave

---

* See Appendix E.

reproaches for the carelessness of his work, and demand back my money ! " *

I quote this specimen of the so-called " scientific " teaching of the 19th century, not so much on account of its gross stupidity, as of its profane blasphemy, as if the most complex and beautiful specimen of the Creator's handywork could be measured or understood by such an Atheist as Helmholtz proved himself to be. If such views had really any hold upon the best and most cultured portion of Christendom, the awful dream of the celebrated John Paul Friedrick Richter, whose portrait was so skilfully drawn by one of your greatest writers in the leading review of the 19th century,† would have become almost a reality—" I wandered to the farthest verge

---

* For an answer to this extraordinary specimen of Atheistic arrogance, see Murphy on *Habit and Intelligence*, i. p. 319.

† Thomas Carlyle, in *Edinburgh Review*, No. 91, 1827. Carlyle is said to have condemned this dogma of the Atheistic school, under the contemptuous epithets of "Deluded Insanity" and "A Gospel of Dirt," &c.

of creation, and there I saw a socket *where an eye should have been,* and I heard the shriek of a fatherless world."

Do not, Gentlemen, suppose for a moment, that I mean to impute any such profane folly to your distinguished Naturalist, Charles Darwin. He was an eminent man, a modest man, and a Christian man; a daring Atheist is necessarily the reverse of all three. But now I must ask your attention to what Darwin taught in his second great work on the origin of the human race, entitled *The Descent of Man.* Here the doctrine of EVOLUTION is stated with great plainness of speech, with charming illustrations of some of your early ancestors, and if it failed in carrying conviction to the wisest and greatest minds of the 19th century, it is not for want of skill in the treatment of the subject by its able and most noted advocate.

The following are Mr. Darwin's confirmed views expressed in his own words: He commences with this frank and candid admission, which does so much honour to himself and the cause he supports: "A large number of naturalists admit that species are the modified descendants of other species; and this especially holds good with the younger and rising natu- lists. The greater number accept the agency of *Natural Selection;* though some urge, whether with justice the future must decide, that I have greatly overrated its importance. *Of the older and honoured chiefs in Natural Science, many,* unfortunately, are still opposed to evolution in every form."*

If he had said "all," in place of "many," I think Darwin would have been nearer the mark so far as regards belief in the chimera that man has been evolved from a tadpole. I shall shew you before I close my address, that almost all the greatest names of the 19th century reject the full bearing of his Evolution theory. Professor Tyndall, the most distinguished of his disciples, admits that it must inevi-

---

* *Descent of Man,* i., pp. 1, 2. It is satisfactory to note the signs which show that the theory of Natural Selection is beginning to break down.

tably undergo "some modification" before it can be accepted by what he considers the scientific world. Darwin's admission that "the older and honoured chiefs" reject it may remind you of an occurrence which took place some 3,000 years ago after the death of the wise King of Israel. The learned and older chiefs advised his successor King Rehoboam one way; "the younger and rising Naturalists" of that period advised him another. He preferred the foolish advice of the latter, and lost half his kingdom thereby.

Nevertheless, Darwin contends with admirable consistency that—"Man is descended from a hairy quadruped, furnished with a tail and pointed ears, probably arboreal in its habits, and an inhabitant of the old world.........The early progenitors of man were no doubt well covered with hair, *both sexes having beards;* their ears were pointed and capable of movement; and their bodies were provided with a tail having the proper muscles.........Their males were provided

with great canine teeth, which served them
as formidable weapons." *

You will observe that Darwin abstains
from accounting for the absence of the tail
in the present race of mankind, or of the
beard in the better and more gentle
female sex. I once met with a reason for the
latter, which I give for what it is worth—
not as my own opinion, but as stated in a
lady's album belonging to the first half of
the 19th century, and who happened to be
one of the most worthy and best of her
sex. The reason given was expressed in
poetic strains to the following effect, that
beards were denied them because (oh! tell
it not in Gath)—

    "*Their tongues would never let their chins be still,*"

were they to require the calm and
placid art of shaving. Nor does he seek
to account for the way in which the race
lost their tails; nor does he attempt to
define the shape of the caudal appendage
which once ornamented the dorsal ex-

---

* See Appendix F.

tremity of prehistoric man. If he meant a quadruped with a *bushy* tail like a horse, he possibly got the idea from a legend once current in Kent, where it was long believed that the inhabitants of Strood, near Rochester, for having insulted the rebel Achbishop Thomas à Becket, by cutting off the tails of his horses, were cursed so vigorously by the angry Primate, that their descendants were ever after *" born with horses' tails !"* *

If, on the contrary, he means a *tufted* tail like the ass, he may have obtained the idea from the exact rendering of Genesis xvi. 12, where it is foretold that Ishmael would be " a wild ass among men."

Professor Huxley, in his *Lay Sermons,* shows that the principal difference between the horse and the ass is two-fold: first, in the ass having callosities in the two fore-legs, whereas the horse has them on all four legs; second, in the former having *a tufted,* while the latter has a bushy tail.

---

* Fuller's *Church History,* ii. 7, § 22.

Notwithstanding that Scripture compares Ishmael to "a wild ass," theDarwinian theory seems to require that the bushy tail of one species of the monkey tribe should be accepted in preference to the *tufted* tail of the ass, as the property of that prehistoric ancestor from which the human race is said to have sprung.

For Mr. Darwin's trumpet gives no uncertain sound, when he thus delivers his testimony respecting the actual line of our primeval ancestors, tracing them back to as far as his theory will allow him to go.

"The most ancient progenitors in the kingdom of the vertebrata at which we are able to obtain *an obscure glance*, apparently consisted of a group of marine animals, resembling *the larvæ of existing ascidians*. These animals *probably* gave rise to a group of fishes, as lowly organized as the lancelet; and from these the ganoids and other fishes like the lepidosiren, must have been developed. From such fish a very small advance would carry us on to the amphibians."

These amphibians, Darwin supposes, gradually developed themselves into reptiles, birds and mammals, so that he judiciously tells you that *no one can at present say by what line of descent* these three higher and related classes sprang from the amphibians, *and* then he proceeds swimmingly as follows:— .

" Birds and reptiles were once intimately connected together, and *the monotremata*, now, *in a slight degree, connect mammals with reptiles.* In the class of *mammals* the steps are *not difficult* to conceive, which led from the ancient monotremata to the ancient marsupials, and from these to the early progenitors of the placental animals. We may thus ascend to the lemuridæ, and the interval is not wide from these to the simiadæ. The simiadæ then branches off into *two great stems, the New World and the Old-World Monkeys*, and from the *latter*, at a remote period, *man, the wonder and glory of the universe, proceeded.* . . . IF a single link in this chain had never existed, man would not have been what he now is.

Unless we wilfully close our eyes, we may, with our present knowledge, approximately recognize our parentage, *nor need we feel ashamed of it.*" *

With these words before us, it is impossible to mistake Darwin's meaning that, in his estimation, man is descended from an old-world monkey, and not, as Scripture teaches, that man was formed out of the dust of the earth by a separate act of creative power, "after the image and likeness of God." And yet when the celebrated Agassiz, equal if not superior to Darwin as a Naturalist, in a lecture at San Francisco, once defined the Evolution theory as an attempt to "determine whether we ourselves are descended from monkeys, or whether we are the work of a beneficent Father," a rash and not very learned disciple of Mr. Darwin had the confidence to write in *Nature*, October 24, 1872, that Agassiz's truthful and necessary conclusions were "singular misrepresentations." ! !

---

* *Descent of Man*, vol. i., pp. 212, 213.

The first thing to observe in Mr. Darwin's pedigree of man is *its extreme length*. His most enthusiastic follower, Professor Huxley, once compared it to that which some Englishmen are fond of boasting about, viz., their descent from some of the Norman robbers, who came over from Normandy with "the Conqueror," as James I.'s witty retort to one of the Lumley family shows. He was boasting that he was descended from a certain "Adam Lumley," who belonged to that piratical crew. "Well, mon, I dinna kno that Adam (referring to him who was expelled from Paradise) was a Lumley"! That curious class of speculators, the so-called "Anglo-Israelites," declare that the English can trace their pedigree from Abraham without a missing link. The noble French family of Montmorenci boast that their founder was a contemporary of Noah, who preserved the archives of the Montmorencies by taking them into the Ark. A certain Welsh chieftain used to display his genealogical tree to his wondering friends, in

the *middle* of which the generation of
Adam appears, thereby proving the Welsh-
man's ancestors as belonging to the class
of pre-Adamites, for which many sciolists
zealously contend in the present day.

But after all what are these to be
compared to the extreme length of the
Darwinian tale, or tail? They are, as the
Yankee acutely said, simply "nowhere."
Let me, however, do full justice to Mr.
Darwin, by calling your attention to what
he teaches respecting your primeval ancestor. You observe that in the passage
already quoted, Darwin can only obtain "*an
obscure glance*" at this ancestor. And so
in another part of the same work he says,
"In the *dim obscurity* of the past, we can
see that the early progenitor of all the
vertebrata must have been an aquatic
animal, provided with brachio, with the
two sexes united in the same individual,
and with the most important organs of the
body (such as the brain and heart)
imperfectly developed. This animal seems
to have been more like *the larvæ of our*

existing ascidians, than any other known form.*

These primeval ancestors of yours are further described by Darwin as " invertebrate, hermaphrodite marine creatures, permanently attached to a support. They hardly appear like animals, and consist of a simple tough, leathery sac, with two small projecting orifices, placed by some Naturalists among the *vermes,* or ' worms.' Their larvæ somewhat resemble tadpoles in shape, and have the power of swimming about " (i. 205). Professor Huxley, in his *Introduction to the Classification of Animals,* says, " They look very much like double-necked jars. At first sight, you might hardly suspect the animal nature of one of these organisms, when freshly taken from the sea; but if you touch it, the stream of water which it squirts out of each aperture reveals the existence of a great contractile power within."

Professor St. George Mivart, in his

---

* *Descent of Man,* ii. 389.

F

Genesis of Species (p. 92), will inform you that these "ascidians are sometimes called *tunicaries*, or sea squirts." And inasmuch as the term *larvæ*, from which Darwin tells you that you are descended, is defined in the Latin dictionary as nothing more or less than "ghosts," it is evident, when speaking with due scientific precision according to the Darwinian philosophy, that the germ of the very original parent of the human race is to be found *in the ghost of a sea squirt!*

Mr. Darwin, while admitting that though he has found for his ancestors "a pedigree of prodigious length," it is "not of a very noble quality," to which you will doubtless give your cordial assent; but when he adds, in the face of Scripture, that "any longer to believe that man is the work of a separate creation" is to adopt the hypothesis of a "savage," you will naturally think who is most like a savage, such men as Bacon, Newton and Milton, three of the greatest intellects which have ever appeared in the world, of whom Cambridge

An Ascidian, or Sea Squirt. The *first* of man's prehistoric
ancestors according to the Darwinian philosophy.

may well be proud, and who bowed to the supremacy of Him who has revealed Himself as the Supreme Creator in His own unerring Word, or that bold speculator who refuses to believe that man is a separate act of creative power, and who appears to be proud of his descent from the ghost of a sea squirt, combined with the form of an old-world monkey.

Professor Huxley describes a remarkable peculiarity belonging to the heart of your ascidian ancestors, which it may be well to notice. He says, "After the heart has been beating a certain number of times in one direction it stops, and then begins beating the opposite way;" [*] in which respect they may be said to resemble the least worthy of their human descendants, who, like rats, invariably desert a sinking ship, and turn heartily to worship the rising sun!

Passing from the earliest of your progenitors according to the Darwinian philo-

_____

[*] *Lay Sermons*, p. 95.

sophy as originally an ascidian tadpole,
or ghost of a sea squirt, to the last of your
prehistoric ancestors as seen in the old-
world monkey, I would direct your attention to what Darwin says about this
important member of your ancestral
pedigree. He has succeeded in finding
the noble and intellectual forehead of man,
together with those facial appointments of
which he is naturally so proud—viz., *beard*,
whisker, and *moustache*—"in the Bonnet
Monkey;" and though he admits that "in
man the nose is much more prominent
than in most monkeys," you may
easily trace the fine old Roman nose—an
"aquiline curvature," as he terms it—in
another of your simian ancestors, the
Horlock Gibbon, which he tells you is there
carried to such a ridiculous extent, as fully
to justify the propriety of the title to one of
the tales of the 19th century, entitled the
Nose with the Man! So Darwin considers
that "the resemblance of the *Pitheca Sata-
nas* (of the monkey tribe, noted for its
magnificent beard and tail), his jet black

A Kahau, or old-world Monkey. The *last* of man's prehistoric ancestors according to the Darwinian philosophy, with ideal human features.

skin, his rolling eye-balls, and hair parted on the top of his head, to a negro in miniature, is almost ludicrous." *

But now two questions arise in connection with this interesting subject. 1st, How did man get rid of the tail which undoubtedly belonged to his early progenitors? And 2dly, Does man still retain the power and capability of bearing the caudal appendage?

The first of these questions may be readily disposed of. The Encyclopædias of the 19th century describe existing ascidians as resembling "tadpoles in shape, and swimming about by means of a vibratile tail, which they *shake off* when they quit the larvæ state, and assume the sitting or fixed condition." If the earliest progenitors of man according to Darwin thus "shook off" his tail when he came of age, and old enough to take his seat in the Legislature of the time, I see no difficulty in supposing that the latest of man's

---

* *Descent of Man*, ii. 382.

prehistoric ancestors did the same; and I am glad to think that this view has the high authority of your great statesman, Mr. Canning, who considered, as I have before pointed out, that the tails of your anthropoid ancestors "gradually rubbed off from long sitting in their caverns or huts." Here I must not omit to mention that Darwin says—"According to popular impression, the absence of a tail is eminently distinctive of man; but as these apes that come nearest to man are destitute of this organ, its disappearance does not specially concern us. Nevertheless, it may be well to own that no explanation, as far as I am aware, has ever been given of the loss of the tail by certain apes and men." *

The second question is not so easily answered, on account of the conflicting evidence which history has brought to light. The *savans*, like doctors, proverbially are at issue on this very point.

---

* *Descent of Man,* i. 150.

One portion declaring that it is impossible for a human being to have a tail, because the spinal vertebræ in the human race do not admit of an elongation, as the spine terminates in the *os sacrum*, thus entirely precluding production or continuation, as in caudate animals. Others assert that the *coccyx*, or lower extremity of the spine, consists of four vertebræ, which in their estimation constitutes a rudimentary tail ; but this is curved forwards, and is not visible externally, an arrangement which is also found in the anthropoid asses and in Hoffman's sloth. It is on this ground, as I conclude, that Darwin confidently asserts that "the *os coccyx*, though functionless as a tail, plainly represents this part in other vertebrate animals; and in certain rare and anomalous cases it has been known, according to Isidore, Geoffry St. Hilaire and others, to form *a small external rudiment of a tail*." *

But now we call History to our aid, and

---

* *Descent of Man*, i. 29.

on the inexorable and logical principle of
facts, which reminds us of Dr. Johnson's
severe remark before quoted respecting
Lord Monboddo's—" Of a standing fact
there ought to be no controversy, sir; if
there are men with tails, they hide them."
True, most learned doctor; but inasmuch
as there are exceptions to every rule, so is it
here.   There are some men who have tails
and do not hide them.   Let the following evidence decide whether such is the
truth or the reverse.   Although you will
naturally be reminded of the old saying
that " travellers tell strange tales (? tails),"
it may be met by another of equal force
that " truth is stranger than fiction; " so
that on the balance of *probabilities*, the
caudal appendage possessed by some of
your early progenitors according to Darwin, has been retained by some of their
unfortunate descendants.   The   ancient
Egyptians, the Assyrians, and the learned
Greeks, prove by their monuments their
belief in the fact.   In the Choragic monument of Lysicrates, on which the adventures

of Bacchus are delineated, all the human figures have tails. In the Cuneiform monument of the Assyrians now in the British Museum, which represents Jehu, king of Israel, paying tribute to Salmaneser II., some of the human figures are adorned with the caudal appendage. So much for the testimony of ancient times.

And if you come down to modern history, you will find the Dutch traveller, John Struys, who visited the Isle of Formosa, near the coast of China, two centuries ago, asserting that the inhabitants there possessed *" tails more than a foot long,* covered with red hair, very like that of a cow."

Colonel du Corret, in a report to the French Academy of Science, declares that when he dwelt at Mecca in 1842, having heard that the Ghilane race had tails, and relating to a friendly Emir how much the *savans* of Europe disbelieved such things, he ordered one of his slaves called "Bellal" to be summoned, when there appeared a thin strong man, about 30 years of age, of the Ghilane tribe, with curly hair, like one of the Positivists, on the top of his head, but no beard—"*his tail was more than three inches long*, and as flexible as that of a monkey."

About the same date, Dr. Joseph Wolff, the famous Jewish Missionary, in his *Travels and Adventures*, says "there are men and women in Abyssinia with *tails like dogs and horses*." And he adds, in confirmation of this strange tale, that "in the College of Surgeons at Dublin may still be seen a human skeleton, *with a tail seven inches long*." *

M. de Castelneau, who visited the same country in 1851, says that "the *Niam-niams* of Abyssinia had all of them *tails* 40 *centimetres long, quite smooth*, and that the women were deformed in the same manner." But his countryman, M. d'Ab-badie, on the authority of an Abyssinian priest, however, contradicts one part of the story by declaring, that "though all

---

* See Appendix G.

the men of the Niam-niams had tails covered with hair, the ladies were very beautiful and *tailless*."

Mr. Francis Gosse, a F.R.S., and therefore worthy of the most implicit credit, as a Fellow of the most scientific Society in England before Darwin was born, notwithstanding De Quincey's epigram,* relates the following story in support of the testimony of the skeleton in the Dublin College of Surgeons, that the ancient Irish were blessed with tails, says " there are in Ireland a few remaining descendants of the people *with tails.* To an old woman, John Cockle, Esq., offered a handsome sum of money for ocular proof of this phenomenon, and on her. refusal attempted to satisfy his curiosity by force; a scuffle ensued, the old woman cried out, which brought her grandsons to her assistance, who beat him most cruelly, and laid an indictment against him for an assault on their grandmother, and it was not

---

* See p. 41.

without considerable expense and trouble that the matter was accommodated." *

All these authorities seem to support the Darwinian theory that men once possessed tails; but that the present race, with some exceptions, resembling angels' visits, " few and far between," no longer has that appendage which in certain animals, like the peacock and bird of Paradise, is so becoming to their personal appearance, and the loss of which some of your *savans* appear to be now so vainly deploring. The successive steps by which Darwin has persuaded himself into the belief of such a remarkable change in the structure of mankind may be briefly noticed here. As his theory depends on proving your descent from some less highly organised form, he points out the presence of certain rudimentary structures in man which connect the human body with many other animals, such as the convoluted substance from which springs the tail of the monkey,

---

* *Essays*, by Francis Gosse, F.R.S., p. 19.

and the blunted point from the folded margin of the ear, which he considers sufficient proof that your ancestors once possessed "pointed ears and a tail."

Then he adduces many interesting traces of correspondence between the ape and yourselves. Amongst others, he mentions a remarkable fact which fully confirms the truth of the schoolboy legend that time was when "monkeys chewed tobacco"—for if they thus treat the fragrant weed, as certain tribes in the far West do who worship a *great red stone pipe*, as part of "their flesh," and esteem it "great medicine" because belonging to their primeval ancestors, and tobacco is pronounced to be "ancestral food,"* it is certain they have adopted the universal practice of their wiser brethren in the far East. Hence, says Darwin—"Many kinds of monkeys have a strong taste for

* See *Prehistoric Man; or Researches into the Origin of Civilisation in the Old and New World*, by Daniel Wilson, LL.D.: 2 vols.; vol. ii., p. 12.

G

tea, coffee and spirituous liquors; they will also, as I have myself seen, smoke *tobacco* with pleasure."* Wild baboons, he adds, are remarkably fond of *beer*, and strange to say when they drink too much, they have a headache next morning, and relish much the piece of lemon, which is perhaps the nearest approach to the brandy-and-water system adopted by fast young men in the 19th century. An instance is on record of a monkey having become so intoxicated with brandy, that he ever after refused to taste a drop; by which act of self-denial, as the great Naturalist justly observes, "he proved himself wiser than many men."

Another argument adduced by Darwin in proof of your descent from the lower animals consists in this:—"Whoever rejects with scorn the belief that the shape of his own canines, and their occasional great development in other men, are due to our early progenitors having been provided

---

* *Descent of Man*, i. 12.

with these formidable weapons, *will probably reveal by sneering at the line of his
descent.*" For though he no longer intends
to use these teeth *as weapons,* he will
unconsciously retract his *snarling muscles,*
so as to expose them ready for action,
like a dog prepared to fight."*

Although this argument from the sneering and snarling muscles of the canine
race is very far from being a proof of your
descent from the lower animals in respect
to such gentle and courteous controversialists as Mr. Charles Darwin, I am
afraid that the argument is peculiarly
applicable to some of his disciples.

An anecdote told of the witty Canon
of St. Paul's, seems in some measure to
support the Darwinian theory of your
canine descent. When the famous painter
of animals, Landseer, offered to paint
his portrait, Sydney Smith rejected the
offer on the same grounds which made
Hazael of Damascus refuse the offer of a

---

* *Descent of Man,* i. 127.

throne—"Is thy servant *a dog*, that he should do this great thing?"

The conclusion of the whole matter at which Mr. Darwin has arrived, respecting the human race having been evolved primarily from a tadpole, and finally from a monkey—seems to rest, not so much upon logical inference, or careful observation, or testing experiment, as upon that exuberant fancy of which he is so great a proficient. You will not therefore be surprised at hearing that having so many undeniable proofs, as he considers, of man's tadpole-cum-monkey descent, he should allow his fancy to lead him thus far astray by declaring that he "would as soon be descended from the heroic little monkey, who braved his dreaded enemy in order to save the life of his keeper; or from that old baboon, who descending from the mountains, carried away in triumph his young comrade from a crowd of astonished dogs; as from a savage who delights to torture his enemies, offers up bloody sacrifices, practices infanticide without remorse, treats his wives like slaves, knows no decency, and is haunted by the grossest superstitions." *

But surely this reasoning partakes more of the imaginative use of science than "the scientific use of the imagination," as the *Times* once remarked of Professor Tyndall's address at Liverpool, for Darwin frequently and his disciples invariably are apt to forget that the real question to be considered before all, is not so much what fancy leads one to imagine in accordance with the previous predisposition, as " *What is true?* " though here I must not forget that one of your learned professors says on a subject on which he is so competent to speak, on the possibility of " spontaneous generation." In his celebrated address as President of the British Association at the Belfast meeting in 1874, after declaring that he " discerns in MATTER the promise and potency of all terrestial life," though he is careful to deny the implication of

---

* *Descent of Man,* ii. 404.

being "a material Atheist," Professor Tyndall says—"If you ask me whether there exists the least evidence to prove that any form of life can be developed out of matter, without demonstrable antecedent life, my reply is that evidence considered by many has been adduced; and that were some of us who have pondered this question to follow a very common example, and accept testimony because it falls in with our belief, we also should eagerly close with the evidence referred. *But there is in the true man of science a wish to have them true.* And this stronger wish causes them to reject the most plausible support, if he has reason to suspect that it is vitiated by error. Those to whom I refer as having studied this question, believing the evidence offered in favour of 'spontaneous generation' to be thus vitiated, cannot accept it" (p. 56).

In the *Nineteenth Century Review*, January and March numbers of 1878, Professor Tyndall has delighted and instructed the world with two most powerful articles in

opposition to the Atheist's claim on behalf
of "spontaneous generation." The professor has on this occasion not only
conclusively proved the truth of Scripture
and Science against the possibility of this
vain conceit of the Materialist, but has
executed his task in such a way, as to offer
a bright example of courtesy towards opponents, which all controversialists in general,
and especially those ardent and fiery souls
of the sacerdotal class in particular, might
profitably follow without injury to their
own cause.

To return, however, to the consideration
of the arguments adduced on behalf of
man being descended from an ascidian
tadpole and an old-world monkey, I must
not omit to notice the important admission
made by Mr. Darwin in the full maturity
of age, and not very long before he died,
viz., that the whole theory of the human
race having been evolved from the larvæ
of an ascidian tadpole, after so many years
of controversial disscussion, is "*only an
hypothesis*," with which every duly qua-

lified person will cordially agree. And
you may have observed in his writings
how commonly the hypothesis of an " If "
is introduced, both by the master and his
numerous disciples. Let me adduce one
specimen as sufficient for our purpose. In
his earlier work on the *Origin of Species*,
Mr. Darwin writes—

" On the principle of Natural Selection
with divergence of character, *it does not
seem incredible* that from some such low
and intermediate form as the lower algæ,
both animals and plants *may have been
developed ;* and IF we admit this, *we must
admit* that all organic beings which have
ever lived on this earth *may have descended*
from some one primordial form." *

An interpreter of Mr. Darwin thus
explains the above passage—" Born of
electricity and albumen, the simple
monod is the first living atom; the
microscopic animalcules, the snail, the
worm, the reptile, the fish, the bird, and

---

* *Origin of Species*, p. 519.

the quadruped, all spring from its invisible loins. The human similitude at last appears in the character of the monkey; the monkey rises into the baboon; the baboon is exalted to the orang outang; and the chimpanzee, with a more human toe and shorter arms, gives birth to man." *

You will have seen how in this extract Mr. Darwin dwells upon the power of the "If." The "ifs," † and the "mays," and the "not incredibles," and the "no difficulties," are modes of expression with which his readers are very familiar. Nor do other distinguished writers refuse to avail themselves of this rather weak support, on which they often raise an imaginative and lofty superstructure: *e.g.*, your celebrated dramatist, in his description of authors' quarrels, speaks of the power of the "If" on this wise :—

"All these you may avoid but the *lie*

---

* *North British Review* of 1845, p. 483.
† See Appendix H.

direct; and you may avoid that too with an IF. I knew when seven justices could not take up a quarrel; but when the parties were met themselves, one of them thought but of an IF, as *If you said so,* then I said so, and they shook hands and swore brothers. Your IF is the only peace-maker, and much value is in an IF."*

In a similar way the famous Pascal contends that "IF Cleopatra's nose had been only a little shorter, the history of the world would have been changed." Victor Hugo adopts the same line of argument respecting the result of Waterloo. "IF it had not rained," he declares, "on the night of the 17th of June, 1815, the future of Europe would have been altered! A few drops of water more or less caused the fall of Napoleon!" Happy conclusion for the vainest of Frenchmen!!!

Much of the Evolutionary hypothesis rests upon this potent "If." Thus one of Darwin's foreign disciples, a noted German

---

* *As You Like It,* act v., scene iv.

Atheist, called Carl Vögt, though slightly differing from the master on the monogonist theory, asserts with surprising confidence, that the *missing link*, for which the whole party have been searching so many years *in vain*, notwithstanding Professor Haeckel's boast that he has discovered it in the "sand-eel," will in due time be discovered, as he thus argues—"IF the macaci of Senegal, the baboons on the Gambia, and the gibbons in Borneo have become developed into Anthropoid apes, *there is no reason why* these different stocks should be denied *the further development into the human type;* in short, I cannot see why American races of men cannot be derived from American apes, Negroes from African apes, or Negritos from Asiatic apes."

Another foreign disciple of Mr. Darwin speaks more positively on the subject, as he discards all reasoning of the "IF" kind. Dr. F. G. Bergmann, in his *Resúme d'Etudes d'Ontologie générale*, projects from the depths of his moral consciousness the beings from which the human race has been evolved. He tells you that their name was *Anthropiskes;* and that *their original dwelling-place was in Central Africa.* These hairy creatures were evolved out of pure "apes," and a certain number of them finding themselves in favourable circumstances, developed into "black men," who became the parents of all the families of the earth, from which the brown, copper, yellow and white races branched off.

Darwin abstains from speaking in the same spirit of Positivism, as is manifested by the French *savant,* which naturally belongs to the countrymen of Comte, for he contents himself with saying, "We do not know whether man is descended from some comparatively small species like the chimpanzee, or from one as powerful as the gorilla," though he cautiously adds that as "it is *probable* Africa was formerly inhabited by extinct apes, closely allied to the gorilla and chimpanzee, and as these two species are now man's *nearest allies,* it is somewhat *more probable* that our *early* *progenitors* lived on the African continent than elsewhere." *

Professor Max Müller explains the difference between the systems of Darwin and one of his German disciples on this wise. The former, he considers, is content with four or five beginnings for all animals and plants ; the latter requires but one primordial cell—a chemical combination of carbon, in the form of *white* of egg, such as *bathybius* from the bottom of the Atlantic in endless varieties. " In this," says Max Müller, with great force of truth, " *there is much ignorance under the form of knowledge.*" †

It will be seen that much of the Evolutionary theory is the product of that system of development from the moral consciousness which is more or less common to all Darwin's disciples, whether English, French or German. It reminds one of Schiller's description of the Alps, without

---

* *Descent of Man,* i. 156, 199.

† See Max Müller's Royal Institution Lecture on the *Relation of Language and Thought.*

his ever having set eyes upon them; and likewise of Goëthe's description of the way in which certain speculators evolve their ideas respecting their supposed ancestors. A Frenchman, an Englishman, and a German were commissioned to give the world the benefit of their views on that lively animal the CAMEL.

Away flew the Frenchman to the *Jardin des Plantes*, spent an hour there in rapid investigation, and then without a moment's delay wrote *currente calamo*, a treatise on the animal, without adding a single idea to man's previous knowledge of Natural History. He was, however, so satisfied with his work, that he was constrained to exclaim in the exuberance of his joy, " *Le voila, le chameau !* "

The Englishman packed up his tea caddy and a store of comforts, pitched his tent in the desert, remained there two years studying THE CAMEL in its habits without order, expounded without philosophy, but serving as valuable materials for all who came after him.

The German, despising the frivolity of the Frenchman, and the unphilosophic matter of the Englishman, retired to his study, there to construct his idea of a camel *from out of the depths of his moral consciousness.* In this characteristic mark of the German mind you may behold the germ and the outcome of the Darwinian philosophy; *i.e.*, of those who go beyond the Master, and who, not content with attributing the first primordial form of life to the act of a divine Creator, adopt the Atheistic theory of Strauss and others, for which he was deservedly reproved by the celebrated HUMBOLT, for stating with most unscientific levity that the ignorganic was capable of evolving organic life, in imitation of the vain and ignorant heathen, though their ignorance was excusable, inasmuch as they were without a revelation from on high.

Thus Justin Martyr, in the 2nd century, relates that some of the boasting *savans* of his day declared that "Mithdras was begotten of *a rock.*" * Other heathen

---

* Justin, *Dial. cum Trypho.*, ch. 70.

believed that men were sprung from *rocks* or *oaks;* while the great Cicero, with that common sense in which the least worthy followers of Darwin in the present day are so manifestly deficient, pointedly declares that " man is *not* chiselled out of the rock, nor hewn out of the *oak;* for he has a soul: the one is actuated by intellect, the other by the senses." *

Yet are some of the supporters of the Evolutionary theory so fanatically opposed to Scripture and common sense, that they contend violently that a *monad* in process of time will become a visible atom, and that by the fortuitous concourse of atoms the worlds were made.

Thus Professor Haeckel teaches that your earliest ancestors, whom he terms " *Monera,*" originated about the beginning of the Laurentian period (the earliest known of the geological strata) by means of spontaneous generation from the so-called

---

* Cicero, *Quæst. Acad.*, iv. 31.

inorganic compounds of carbon, hydrogen, oxygen, and nitrogen."* And in his Munich address, the same Professor affirms that "the *monera*, consisting of *protoplasm* only, bridge over the deep chasm between organic and inorganic nature, while they show *how* the simplest and oldest organisms *must have* originated from *inorganic carbon compounds*." Just as he supposes elsewhere that the sand-eel bridges over the equally "deep chasm" between man and monkey!!! Haeckel is so satisfied of the truth of his theory, that he asserts again and again that *monera*, worms and fishes were our early progenitors. Misreading or incapacity to understand the figurative language of Scripture, leads men into sad blunders; as, *e.g.*, where the afflicted patriarch cries, "I have said to corruption, Thou art my father: to the *worm*, Thou art my mother and my sister."† Haeckel teaches that "*without any*

---

* Haeckel's *Natürliche Schöpfungsgeschichte*, p. 578.
† Job xvii. 14.

H

doubt a long series of extinct worms were our direct ancestors"! ! [*]

Professor Huxley is so enamoured of the Evolutionary theory, whether as taught by the Atheistic Haeckel, or the more sober-minded Christian, Darwin, that while he contents himself with placing the latter on a par with Newton, he declares of the former that "whether one agrees or disagrees with him, one feels that he has forced the mind into lines of thought in which it is *more profitable to go wrong than to stand still*"!

Hence he says, "To put Haeckel's views into a few words, he conceives that all forms of life originally commenced as *monera*, or simple particles of protoplasm; and these "monera originated from non-living matter." [†]

It is often said there is but one step from the sublime to the ridiculous; a saying peculiarly apposite to the various

---

[*] *Anthropogenie, p.* 39 9
[†] Huxley's *Critiques and Addresses,* p. 314.

theories broached by Darwin's disciples respecting the origin and the pedigree of your race, as contrasted with the simple, truthful, and dignified manner in which it is recorded in the only Book which has God for its author, truth without mixture of error for its matter, and the happiness of mankind for its end; where you may learn for certain that man was created from the dust of the earth by the fiat of the Almighty in the image and likeness of God.

Contrast this with the palpable absurdities and infidel theories invented by ancient and modern philosophers respecting the origin of man. In the *Symposiacs* of Plutarch, you will find a discussion whether man grew out of a *rock* or an *oak*, which has been renewed 18 centuries later by your speculators of the present day, who believe, or say they believe, that man has "grow'd," like Topsy, from a bed of weeds, which came in its turn originally, Professor Huxley will tell you, from an atom of PROTOPLASM. An anecdote

is recorded in the literature of your black
brethren of America, which is very ap-
propriate to this hazy notion of man's
primeval ancestor. A Negro Debating
Society once met to discuss the following
question—"Which am de mudder ob de
chicken—de hen wot lay de egg, or de
hen wot hatches de chick?" After a
warm debate, when the majority seemed
disposed to adopt the maternity of the
latter, an intelligent Darkey among the
minority arose, and made a proposition
to the following effect. Said he, "S'pose
dat you set one dozen duck's eggs under
a hen, and dey hatch; which am de
mudder, de duck or de hen?" This was
a poser, but the President, who sided
with the majority, was equal to the
occasion. So after scratching his woolly
pate for an idea, he rose with becoming
dignity, and in all the pride of conscious
superiority announced his decision as
follows:—"Ducks am not before de
house; chicken am de question; derefore
I rule de ducks out!" And so he did,

to the complete discomfiture of his opponents.

Mr. Darwin, however, was so confident of the truth of his theory respecting man having been evolved from an ascidian tadpole and an old-world monkey, that he boasted that—

"The grounds upon which this conclusion rests *will never be shaken*, for the close similarity between man and the lower animals in *embryonic development*, &c., the rudiments which he retains, and the abnormal reversions to which he is occasionally liable, are facts which cannot be disputed. The great principle of EVOLUTION stands up clear and firm, when these groups of facts are considered in connexion with others; all point to the conclusion that man is the co-descendant with other mammals of a common ancestor .... Man is developed from an ovule about the 125th of an inch in diameter, which differs in no respect from the ovules of other animals. The embryo itself at a very early period, can hardly be distinguished from other members of the vertebrate kingdom." *

Darwin appears to have forgotten the judge's sage advice to an enquirer, "Give your opinion, but never give your reason for forming that opinion; " for when he grounds his theory on the fact that the ovule of a dog (much smaller than a small pin's head) and a human ovule are very similar, he appears to be oblivious of the fact that *the ovule of a dog always produces a dog, while the human ovule never produces a dog but always a man.* Whereas if there existed that perfect resemblance which Darwin fancies he detects between the two, they ought to be capable of producing indifferently dogs or donkeys, monkeys or men! Hence the foremost Palæontologist of the 19th century, whose authority on Natural History stands at a higher elevation than all Mr. Darwin's disciples put together, I refer to Professor OWEN, positively asserts that "the em-

---

* *Descent of Man,* i. 14.

bryo of man does not pass through the lower forms of animals."

In the same spirit another high authority of the 19th century, Professor Max Müller, in his third Lecture on Darwinism at the Royal Institution, when his special subject was *The Relation of Language and Thought*, forcibly observed that "as it was impossible for him to say that man has or may have been developed from some lower animal, it seemed to him to be *the duty of every friend of truth to resist with all his might the hasty conclusions of the Darwinian school*, and to remind its triumphant disciples that nothing is so dangerous to the quiet pursuit of truth as popular applause. As far as we can trace back the footsteps of man, even in the lowest strata of history, we see that the Divine gift of a sound and sober intellect belonged to him from the very first, and the idea of a humanity emerging slowly from the depths of an animal brutality can *never be maintained again*."

To the above opinions, so subversive of

Mr. Darwin's hypothesis, I would add the
testimony of another eminent authority
of that age, in the person of Professor
CLERK-MAXWELL, as set forth in his Lecture
delivered at Bradford in 1873. "Nothing
of EVOLUTION," he declares, "can be
formed to account for the similarity of
molecules, for Evolution necessarily implies
continuous change, and the molecule is
incapable of growth or decay, of generation
or destruction. . . . Science is incompetent
to reason on the creation of matter itself
out of nothing. We have reached the
utmost limit of our thinking faculties,
when we have admitted that because
matter cannot be eternal and self-existent
it must have been created."

Such is the answer which the true men
of science of the 19th century have made
to the unscientific follies and crude speculations of men like Lucretius in ancient
times, and Oken in modern, when they
taught that the origin of all things was
nothing! It is scarcely necessary to say that
Mr. Darwin never lent his countenance to

such puerile vanities as these; though many of his unworthy disciples, who traded upon his great name, played sufficient pranks about matter and the power of atoms enough to make angels weep at the degradation to which they would fain reduce man, made after the image and likeness of God!

Hence a noted German Atheist, of the name of Dr. Louis Büchner, who claims to have published views identical with those of Darwin seven years before *The Origin of Species* saw the light,* declares with equal confidence and candour, that such opinions "are perfectly irreconcilable with the idea of a personal Almighty Creative power, which could not have adopted such a slow and gradual labour, and have rendered itself dependent upon the natural phases of the development of the earth."†

Although Darwin has not the Atheistic

---

* See Appendix I.

† *Kraft und Stoff*, "Force and Matter," p. 84.

difficulty to overcome, as so many of his
disciples appear to have, he has sufficient
of his own, in the attempt to uphold the
Evolution theory, which admits the one act
of the Creator in calling Life into existence,
when he supplements it by the hypothesis
of the Transmutation of one species into
another.   And which one of his opponents,
about a quarter of a century ago, fore-
seeing the impossibility of such a theory
(as a human infant being born, which had
not a human parentage) being true, thus
effectually pointed his shaft at a theory,
some parts of which Darwin frankly acknowledged to be absurd in the highest
possible degree: " It does appear strange
that any Naturalist should ever have upheld
so monstrous a doctrine as that of *the
transmutation of one species into another*. . .
The whole theory is full of inconsistencies
from beginning to end; and from whatever
point we view it, it is equally unsound." *

* Woolaston, *Op. Cit.*, pp. 186, 188 ; A.D. 1856.
Dedicated to Mr. Darwin.

In the same strain Dr. Bree has proved
that Darwin's *Theory of Natural Selection*
"attributes, every thing to chance. An
imaginary power takes the place of *design;*
a series of imaginary laws, which have no
congruity, take the place of the laws of
life; wild speculation is made to supersede
proof, and the proof that is tendered is
founded upon a false interpretation of
facts, or facts have been imagined to replace realities. From beginning to end
Darwin's *Origin of Species* is a cheerless,
gloomy narrative. It destroys every vestige from the mind, without replacing it,
without even a plausible or intelligent
theory." *

By this wonderful theory of Natural
Selection, that old gossiping chronicler,
Giraldus Cambriensis, relates a medieval
myth of the 12th century, how that an
Irishman was transmuted into a salmon;
in the same way, I suppose, that Professor
Huxley declares that by eating mutton

---

* Dr. Bree's *Species Not Transmutable,* p. 254.

sheep are transmuted into men by "an inward laboratory, which dissolves a portion of the modified protoplasm" which passes into the veins, and its "subtle influences convert the dead protoplasm into living protoplasm." In the same way, by supping on lobster, "the matter of life of the crustacean undergoes the same wonderful metamorphosis into humanity." * Thus on the same principle, Darwin's wonderful bear, when engaged in fly-fishing with his mouth wide open, becomes gradually transmuted into the great mammalia of the seas, the spermaceti whale!

If we wish to know the answer which science makes to this charming nonsense, which proved so captivating to the speculating professors of the 19th century, I would remind you of the two unalterable laws in Nature, which forbid the possibility of this fanciful theory being true. *First*— The law of *avitism*, which limits variation by parental peculiarity. Secondly—The

---

* Huxley, *On the Physical Basis of Life*, p. 146.

law of *hybridism,* which being in itself a
limited confusion of nature, bears in itself
a barrier to the extension of that confusion
in the well-known fact that hybrids cease
to breed their like. If, therefore, a law
could be found whereby Transmutation of
Species, either by Natural Selection or
protoplastic conjuring, or any other means,
could be promoted, there is a law to pre-
vent change of kind; and the one is totally
incompatible with the other.

Hence, one of the greatest authorities of
the 19th century, perhaps the most distinguished of the foreign Naturalists of
this age, and happily free from that dangerous spirit of speculation which caused
so much injury to the interest of science
at that time, has truly pointed out, that
however closely the processes of development may " approach or cross each other,
they never end in making any living being
different from the one which gave it birth
though reaching in that point it may
pass through phases resembling other animals . . . . So called varieties or breeds,

far from indicating the beginning of new types, or the initiating new species, only point out the range of flexibility in types, which in their essence are invariable." *

In another work the same great Naturalist points out, while admitting the manifest progress in the succession of all beings on the face of the earth, in the increasing similarity to the living fauna, and among the vertebrates especially in their increasing resemblance to man, that "this connection is not the consequence of a direct lineage between the fauna of different ages. There is nothing like parental descent connecting them. *The fishes of the Palæozoic age are in no respect the ancestors of the reptiles of the secondary age, nor does man descend from the mammals which preceded him in the tertiary age.* The link by which they are connected is of a higher and immaterial nature; and their connection is to be sought in the view of the Creator Him-

---

* Agassiz, *Travels in Brazil*, pp. 41, 42.

self, whose aim in forming the earth and in allowing it to undergo the successive changes which Geology has pointed out, and in creating successively all the different types of animals which have passed away, was to introduce man upon its surface. Man is the end towards which all the animal creation has tended from the first appearance of the first Palæozoic fishes." *

I am not aware that any attempt has ever been made, either by Darwin himself, or by any of his disciples, to answer Agassiz on this point. In which respect they have, according to the usual practice of ardent, but ill-informed controversialists, shown their discretion by ignoring the conclusive arguments of their opponents.

Another of the celebrities of the 19th century, Professor ST. GEORGE MIVART, has well remarked concerning the theory of Natural Selection, that " the special Darwinian hypothesis is beset with certain scientific difficulties, which the author

---

* Agassiz, *Comparative Anatomy*, §§ 689, 90.

ventures to think are absolutely *insuper-able*," just as the late Bishop Phillpotts pronounced the differences between the Churches of England and Rome to be; *
because, as he proves—"Natural Selection is incompetent to account for the incipient stages of useful structures; and does not harmonise with the co-existence of closely similar structures of diverse origin; and some facts of geographical distribution intensify other difficulties; and the objection drawn from the physiological difference between 'species' and 'races' still exist unrefuted."† Professor Mivart somewhat severely remarks, that "it was inevitable that very many half-educated men and shallow thinkers should accept with eagerness the theory of *Natural Selection*, or rather what they think to be such (for few things are more remarkable

---

* See his *Letters to the late Charles Butler*, "On the Insuperable Difficulties which Separate the Church of England from the Church of Rome." New Edition, 1866.

† See Appendix J.

than the manner in which it has been misunderstood), on account of a certain characteristic it has in common with other
theories, which should not be mentioned in
the same breath with it, except, as now,
with the accompaniment of protest and
apology " (p. 12).

According, therefore, to Darwin's theory
of Natural Selection, each of the successive
races of man's progenitors, from the hairy
quadruped to man himself, must have been
better fitted to maintain its position in the
world than any which preceded it. There is,
however, this conclusive answer, which is
fatal to Darwin's theory; viz., that while
many monkey tribes survive, all the
anthropomorphous, or man-shaped apes,
have entirely perished. Here you have
a striking instance of *facts contradicting
theories;* and shows the exceedingly weak
point of Mr. Darwin's reasoning. For
according to his hypothesis, the survival
of the fittest is a necessary part of his
theory; according to the inexorable logic of
facts, the fittest apes have all perished, and

I

the missing link, to the great chagrin of Darwin, never has been, and you may rest assured never will be, found. Hence he is unwillingly constrained to admit, that *" the great break in the organic chain between man and his nearest allies,* which cannot be bridged over by any . extinct or living species, *has often been advanced as a grave* (? insuperable) *objection to the belief that man is descended from some lower form."**

I am aware that Darwin asserts that "this objection will not appear of much weight to those who believe in the general principle of Evolution;" but this is because he treats with singular levity all the evidence to be derived from revelation, tradition, observation, experience, experiments, the reasoning of philosophers—in short, any thing and every thing which militates against his pet theory. This habit of wilfully closing his eyes against all evidence has caused him to be compared to a horse with his blinkers on,

---

* *Descent of Man,* i., p. 200.

the difference between his supposed quadruped ancestor being simply this— that men put blinkers on their horses in order to have them more under their controul, and to constrain them to look only in one direction; Mr. Darwin puts them on himself, thus excluding the light of evidence around him, and compelling him to confine his vision to the one narrow line along which he alone permits himself to look.

Although Darwin freely acknowledges that his views on the Evolution theory, or the descent of man from an ascidian tadpole and an old-world monkey, need not hurt the religious views of any one, he did not probably realize how many religious persons there are who believe that Scripture really means what it says in relation to the origin of man. Believing that the Scripture language is to be understood in its natural sense, it certainly appears to teach, 1st, that man was a separate act of creative power; and, 2nd, that all mankind are sprung from a single pair, like Adam and Eve, who were created after the image and likeness of their Maker.

On the first head Darwin tells his readers in *The Origin of Species*, he "had two distinct objects in view—1st, To show that species had *not* been separately created; and, 2nd, That Natural Selection had been the chief agent of change." In his later work on the *Descent of Man*, he explains himself more fully by saying that if he had "erred in giving to *Natural Selection* great powers, which he is far from admitting, or in having exaggerated its power, which is in itself *probable*, he hopes that he has done good service in aiding to overthrow *the dogma of separate creations*;"* *i.e.*, in other words, according to those who believe in the supremacy and infallibility of the Bible, in endeavouring to prove the Bible to be untrue.

Mr. Darwin's denial of man being a

---

* *Descent of Man*, i., pp. 152, 3.

separate act of creative power should rather be termed an "*hypothesis*" than a "*dogma;*" but in his reasoning on the subject he appears to make little or no distinction between the two terms. For his mode of procedure appears to be somewhat as follows. First he imagines something on the principle of Professor Tyndall's "Scientific Use of the Imagination," or rather the imaginative use of science; then he thinks he sees it; afterwards that others see it as well as himself. Finally, he considers it proved, and writes it down as a scientific fact, and thus builds up his hypothesis, and dignifies it by the name of DOGMA; forgetful of the wise words with which the *Times* (October 3rd, 1876) criticised Tyndall's Discourse on the "Scientific Use of the Imagination," delivered before the British Association at Liverpool, when the critic described it as "an argument of no common order," in which the professor concluded "with an appeal of unrivalled eloquence to *abandon dogmatism for ever*, and fairly to bring every hypothesis before the bar of a disciplined reason."

Mais revenons à nos moutons, as the French phrase it, though not in reference to your *sheepish* ancestors according to the transubstantiation theory of Professor Huxley, I would again remind you of the wonderful powers claimed for the *Evolution theory* and *Natural Selection* by Darwin and his disciples. We have seen how the master is enabled by this means to change bears into whales. Hence one of his disciples explains with scientific precision how your domestic cattle have acquired their horns.

" Let us suppose," says Strauss, " a herd of cattle in primitive times to be still destitute of horns (like the polled cattle in Suffolk), only possessed of powerful necks and projecting foreheads. The herd is attacked by beasts of prey: it defends itself by running against them, and butting with the head. Should this butting in an individual have developed into an incipient horny accretion, then such an individual would have the best chance of preserving his existence (survival of the fittest theory). If the less equipped bulls of the herd were torn to pieces, then the individual thus equipped would propagate the species. Then little by little a completely horned species would be formed, especially if the other sex would of its own accord give the preference to the males thus ornamented, and here Darwin's theory of NATURAL SELECTION is supplemented by the so-called Sexual Selection, to which he has recently devoted a special work."

In a similar manner another of Darwin's distinguished disciples, Sir John Lubbock, in his address at York in 1881, as President of the British Association, committed the common fault of treating as scientific truths the *Evolution* and *Natural Selection* theories, which were even then warmly disputed or denied by almost all the chief authorities of that age, as I shall presently show; and which have by this time, as you yourselves well know, totally disappeared, "having melted," as Professor Tyndall has quaintly phrased it, " into the infinite azure of the past."

Hence Sir John Lubbock was venturesome enough to declare that the science of his time had made such surprising progress, that he was enabled to " see at a glance that the *stripes* of a tiger have reference to its life among *jungle grasses;* that the lion is *sandy* like the *desert;* while the *markings* of the leopard resemble *spots of sunshine* glancing through the leaves ! "

I am inclined to think that the British Association of 1881 must have fallen to a very low ebb from its original formation half a century before, when its President could have adopted such wild reasons, and such almost ludicrous speculations to account for the stripes of the tiger or for the colour of the lion's skin ! Sir John Lubbock might have as well argued that the skin of cattle and sheep ought to be *green*, since they are always feeding on grass ; or you may ask why he hesitated to describe the remarkable scenery, which a similar

"glance" would be required for the production of a *piebald horse* ! For as the Rev.
F. O. Morris, one of the first authorities of
that age on the subject of birds, justly
commented on the President's strange hal-
lucination, in somewhat severe terms,—
" As a matter of fact, the lion does *not* live
in the sandy desert, but in the dense
jungle, amidst an infinity of colours of the
brightest hues ; and when he comes out
into the open desert of sand, if it be sand,
it is at night, when the colour of neither
can have any effect whatever one way or
another."

A notable instance of the progress of
Atheism, as well as of the difficulties
which the *Evolution theory* in place of
solving is sure to create, occurred at the
same meeting of the British Association,
when Professor Seeley had finished reading his paper on the development of
the *plesiosaurus* from the *simosaurus-
pusillus*, Dr. Wright forcibly remarked that
" the professor ought to have gone further, and showed the wondrous adapta-

tions of the Creator, so that their thoughts might be raised beyond the consideration of *dry bones*." To which appeal Professor Seeley candidly replied—" If *design* in anatomy were accepted, there would be an end of all philosophic anatomy. *The whole science of Evolution had grown out of the abandonment of this notion of design.*"

Such was the blindness of scientific infidelity towards the close of the 19th century, unable or unwilling to admit the force of teleology, or the argument from design, as a sure proof of the existence of an all-wise Supreme Creator. He who is unable to admit the overwhelming evidence in proof of an Omnipotent Designer, as witnessed, for example, in the creation of the carboniferous era solely for the use of man long ages after it was made, or the formation of that complex organ called "the eye," whether of man or beast, but prefers to attribute them to his ideal deity of Force, or Matter, or the fortuitous concourse of atoms, is guilty of an "ab-

surdity in the highest possible degree,"
as Darwin expressed it, or of a species
of "deluded insanity," as Carlyle rightly
termed it; and he likewise fulfils in his
own individual person what one far greater
than either Darwin or Carlyle said 3000
years ago, in the words of the inspired
Psalmist—"The fool hath said in his
heart, There is no God." Happy would it
have been for Professor Seeley if he could
have realized the force of the observation
made by Professor PHILLIPS, Secretary of
the British Association at its formation,
to the following effect: "No one who
has advanced so far in philosophy as to
have thought of one thing in relation
to another, *will ever be satisfied with laws
which had no author, works which had no maker,
and co-ordinations which had no designer.*"
Nevertheless, it is certain that the Ultra-
montanes among the Evolutionists go the
lengths of teaching that dead inorganic
matter is capable of evolving organic
life. The illustrious founder of the
Evolution theory rejected the idea with

horror, but many of his Atheistic disciples, undeterred by its blank materialism, far exceeded the speculations of the master: *e.g.*, Dr. Louis Bückner, a noted German Naturalist, but one of the "weaker brethren," according to Professor Tyndal's theory, has declared in his work on *Force and Matter*, that respecting Evolution "the *law of analogy was perfectly irreconcilable with the idea of a personal Almighty power.*"

Such was the materialistic infidelity of the 19th century, less gross, but more pernicious to the young and thoughtless than that of the 18th, which attained to the climax of blasphemy when a fanatical comedian of the name of Monvel, during the saturnalia of the first French Revolution, burst out in a paroxysm of Atheistic fury, exclaiming in the Church of St. Roch—"God! if you exist, avenge your injured name! I bid you defiance; you remain silent, you dare not launch your thunders! *Who after this will believe in your existence?*" *

---

* Alison's *History of Europe*, ch. xiv., § 48.

One of the most eminent preachers of the 19th century, the celebrated ROBERT HALL, in striking contrast to Professor Huxley, the author of *Lay Sermons*, has forcibly described in his own powerful language the difference between the bold Atheism of the French Revolutionists and the cultured infidelity of sceptical *savans* who appeared in the 19th century. After mentioning that Hume, Bolinbroke and Gibbon addressed themselves exclusively to the higher classes, he adds—"Infidelity has lately grown condescending; bred in the speculations of a daring philosophy, immured at first in the cloisters of the learned, and afterwards nursed in the lap of voluptuousness and of courts, having at length reached its full maturity, it boldly ventures to challenge the suffrages of the people, and solicits the acquaintance of peasants and mechanics, and seeks to draw whole nations to its standard. But infidelity is an evil of short duration. It has no individual subsistence given it in the system of prophecy. It is not a *Beast*, but a mere putrid excrescence of the Papal Beast—an excrescence which, though it may diffuse death through every vein of the body on which it grew, yet shall die along with it. Its enormities will hasten its overthrow. It is in no shape formed for perpetuity."

Nothing is more surprising than the poverty of argument displayed, and the illogical train of reasoning adopted by those of Mr. Darwin's disciples, who ignore or deny alike the God of Revelation and the Creator of the Universe. It will be sufficient if I remind you of the opinions of some of the most learned scientists of the 19th century in opposition to these Atheistic delusions. "We need not," said Professor MAIN, once Radcliffe Observer at Oxford, "in accepting the Biblical narrative of man's creation, repudiate one fact accurately deduced from modern scientific research."

In the same strain wrote Professor CHALLIS, Plumian Professor at Cambridge—

"The language of Scripture neither is nor can be contrary to the language of Science."

And so Professor STOKES, Secretary of the Royal Society—"The Book of Nature and the Book of Revelation come alike from God, and consequently there can be no discrepancy between the two, if rightly interpreted." Likewise Professor PORTER, of Belfast, most truly declared that—"Not a single fact of Science fully ascertained, has ever yet been proved to be in opposition to a single statement of Scripture rightly understood."

The great gulf between Darwin and his Atheistic followers was seen in this, that the master was content with the Evolution theory to conceive, though "only as an hypothesis," that it was possible for the ovilia to develop themselves into the mammalia, and monkeys into men; while the disciples plunged into the slough of materialism; rushing like madmen where "angels feared to tread," and boldly contending that inorganic azoic matter could and did develop itself first into living organisms, and finally into man, "the wonder and glory of the universe," as Mr. Darwin says, or as better expressed in the language of Moses, "made after the image and likeness of God."

The whole question, then, resolves itself into this—Creation or Evolution? Which is true? It is impossible to reconcile them. All argument from observation and experience are distinctly in favour of the one, and consequently adverse to the other. No single case of Evolution from one species to another has ever been produced. If there has, as Dr. Johnson said of Lord Monboddo, the original propounder of Darwin's theory, let him produce a specimen of man with a tail; so you may challenge the whole Darwinian party to produce a single specimen of one species developing itself into another—though Darwin has supposed it possible that a bear swimming about with its mouth wide open trying to catch flies, would, if it swam long enough, and kept its mouth wide open all the time, gradually be transmuted into a creature as large as a whale!

Joking, however, apart, I may remind you that there are many insuperable bars to even the modified idea of a monkey growing like Topsy into a man, which may summarily be expressed under these three heads—

1. Articulate Language.
2. Improvable Reason.
3. Moral Responsibility.

On the first of these heads Darwin says—"Articulate language is peculiar to man; but he uses it in common with the lower animals, in articulate cries to express his meaning, aided by gestures and the movements of the muscles of the face. But it is not the mere power of articulation that distinguishes man from other animals, for, as every one knows, parrots can talk; but it is his large power of connecting definite sounds with definite ideas, and

K

this obviously depends on the development of the mental faculties."*

Notwithstanding this frank admission respecting one of the many great gulfs between man and monkey on the subject of language, Darwin seems so scared with the idea that it may tend to subvert his idolised theory, that though he gives several pages to the subject generally, he carefully omits all consideration of the one crucial point—viz., the peculiarity which he owns distinguishes man from other animals—"his large power of connecting definite sounds with definite ideas." Hence he contents himself with one of his usual probabilities—"Some early progenitor of man may *probably* have used his voice largely, as does one of the gibbon-apes of the present day in producing musical cadences"—adding that "mon-

* *Descent of Man,* i., p. 54. It was a fine saying of the celebrated Humboldt, that "Man is man only by means of speech, but that in order to invent speech, he must be man already." Quoted by Sir Charles Lyell in his *Antiquity of Man,* p. 468.

keys certainly understand much that is said to them by man, and utter signal cries of danger to their fellows," in which Mr. Darwin thinks he has found " a first step in the formation of language."*

It is unnecessary to remind you how directly this conflicts with the account given by Moses of the creation of man after the image of God, perfect in every respect, and endowed with the gift of speech and reason, as well as being conscious of right and wrong, as seen in the record of the fall.

Although Darwin is reticent on the point already mentioned, not so one of his disciples, and that one being a cleric of a very rare kind, quite a *rara avis in terris*, a suspended parson convicted of unorthodox speculations. The Rev. Dunbar Heath, M.A., F.R.S.L., F.A.S.L., in a paper read before the Anthropological Society, *On the Acquirement of Language by Mutes*, relates that after having investigated the subject

---

* *Descent of Man*, i., pp. 54—7.

from a scientific standpoint, he concluded
that your human ancestors in Europe must
have been *mutes !* Though he adds somewhat paradoxically, that these *mutes* possibly possessed the power of speech, observing, " I wish my readers to understand that by mute men I mean men who
may or may not use words, but who only
express emotions, and that such emotions
are the individual *emotions* of the mute
being . . . . . . The scientific evidence in
favour of the traditional (*i.e.,* Biblical)
view being *absolutely none at all of any kind
whatever*, I compare it therefore *unfavour-
ably* with the other view now rising into
public notice. This view is, that during
and after the tertiary and geological epoch,
the highest mammals then on earth were
becoming more and more erect in their
way of walking, less hairy in their bodies,
and more like in general to what the
lowest men are now. Such beings are
supposed during these changes to have
also gradually *rationalised some of their
emotions*, by the use of mental powers,

though not so much beyond what the average of them possessed as to suppose a *miraculous development*."

Mr. Heath then proceeds to account for the formation of articulate language. He depicts a small band of six well-armed and speaking Aryans coming suddenly upon a crowd of what he calls mute "kitcheners," and imposing their language on these unfortunate mutes. "Now follow," he says, "the leader of the six Aryans in his first lesson, to the crowd of 300 mutes around him. Naturally he would get the crowd to pronounce after him some short syllables, such as *pa*, *ta*, *ka*, to illustrate the use of lips, palate and throat, and very naturally the four or five men, or *women more likely*, just in front of him would pronounce them rightly, but not one man in fifty can tell the real effect of his work on a crowd. On returning to their wigwams, much would be the *emotion of risibility and imitativeness* displayed that night among the natives!" Doubtless!

The same speculating cleric in the

Anthropological Review, No. xiii., explains how the Aryans first acquired the power of speech, which they subsequently taught to the mute kitchen-middeners. He supposes that at one time Europe abounded with apes, " the fathers" of European men, who were at first dumb, but who in time, by *gasping after articulation*, at length obtained it. " I confine myself to the accepting and explaining known and knowable phenomena. It is *known* that anthropoids existed throughout Europe. It is *knowable* that they became mute men. It is knowable that these mutes *gasped after articulation*, and in a few spots attained to it. Those who did so at one particular spot I call *Aryans*, whether that spot was in Asia or in the submerged continent of Atalantis ! "

As a contrast to this teaching respecting the origin of speech and language in man, I would ask your attention to one who may fairly be termed the first authority of the 19th century on Philology—I refer to Professor Max Müller. In the fourth volume of his interesting work, *Chips from a German Workshop*, you will find a paper entitled, "*My Reply to Mr. Darwin;*" in which the learned professor, after paying a well-deserved compliment to the author of the *Origin of Species*, observes on that famous book—"To me, the few pages devoted to language by Mr. Darwin were full of interest, as showing the conclusions to which that school of philosophy, which he so worthily represents, is driven with regard to the nature and origin of language. I do not think there would be any thing offensive in stating that Mr. Darwin, sen., knows the results of the science of language *at second hand*, and that his opinions on the subject, however interesting as coming from him, cannot be accepted or quoted as authoritative. It has often done infinite mischief when men who have acquired a right to speak with authority on one subject, express opinions on other subjects with which they are but slightly acquainted." *

---

* *Chips*, iv., p. 435.

On the important subject of the Evolution theory, Professor Max Müller justly remarks—"The question is not whether the belief that animals so distinct as a man, a monkey, an elephant, and a humming bird, a snake, a frog, and a fish could all have sprung from the same parents is monstrous, but solely and simply *whether it is true.*" *

On the subject of language, Max Müller observes—"In his *Lectures on Language,* Professor Whitney protests strongly against Darwinian materialism. But as he confesses himself half a convert to the *bow-wow* and *pooh-pooh* theories,† thus showing how wrong I was in supposing that those theories had no advocates among comparative philologists in the 19th century—nay, as now, after he has discovered at last that I am no believer in *Dingdongism,* he seems inclined to say a kind word for the advocates of that theory, Heyse and Steinthal, who

---

* *Chips,* iv., p. 451.   † See Appendix K.

knows whether, after my Lectures on Darwin's *Philosophy of Language*, he may not be converted by Bleek and Haeckel, 'the mad Darwinian,' as he calls him." *

With justice Max Müller continues—"Why is there all this wrangling as to whether man is the descendant of a lower animal or not? Why cannot people examine the question in a temper more consonant with real love of truth?... Let us see what exists to day. We see to day that the lowest of savages, men whose language is said to be no better than the clucking of hens, or the twittering of birds, and who have been declared in many respects lower even than animals, possess this one *specific characteristic*, that if *you take one of their babies, and bring it up in England, it will learn to speak as well as any English baby, while no amount of education will elicit any attempts at language from the highest*

---

* *Chips*, iv., p. 469.

animals, whether bipeds or quadrupeds. That disposition cannot have been formed by definite nervous structures, congenitally framed, for we are told by the best Ayriologists that both father and mother clucked like hens. The fact, therefore, unless disproved by experiment, remains, whatever the explanation may be." *

This is one of the many conclusive proofs against the theory of man's descent from the lower animals being true. The professor then concludes his *Reply to Mr. Darwin* with these instructive words— " We cannot be reminded too often that all the materials of our knowledge we share with animals; that, like them, we begin with sensuous impressions, and then, like ourselves, *and like ourselves only*, we can rise superior to our bestial self, and strive after what is unselfish, good and God-like. .... Let us take continual care, especially within the precincts of the Temple of Science, lest by abusing the gift of

* See Appendix L.

speech or doing violence to the voice of conscience, we soil the two wings of our soul, and fall back, through our own fault, to the dreaded level of the Gorilla."*

These are wise words, and in the above quotations you will observe how justly Max Müller condemns the use of violent language in controversy, and how carefully he avoids committing such a fault himself. It may be accepted as an infallible rule that he who indulges in such a mode of controversy is generally in the wrong. And the intolerant dogmatism which some of the disciples of Darwin have assumed, in direct opposition to the practice and principles of the master, may be judged from the violent language employed by them towards opponents who reject their wild speculations about God and man. Professor Haeckel divides mankind into two classes, "the thoughtful and the thoughtless,"— the former, who accept his doctrines; the latter who do not; while he affirms that

---

* *Chips*, iv., p. 472.

those who do not believe his version of the
doctrine of Evolution, are "for the most
part either ignorant or superannuated."*
Professor Huxley pronounces his opponents
to be "persons who not only have not attempted to go through the discipline necessary to enable them to be judges, but who
·have not even reached that stage of emer-
gence from ignorance, in which the knowledge that such a discipline is necessary
dawns upon the mind." † Dr. Louis
Büchner calls those who take a different
view from himself as "mental slaves"—
"speculative idiots"—"yelping curs;"
while he prematurely boasts of his own
"enlightenment, and the forthcoming de-
liverance of his fellow-men from obsolete
and pernicious prejudices." ‡

It has been justly said that it would be
difficult to find any instance of theological

* *Natürliche Schöpfungsgeschichte*, pp. 577, 638. Elsewhere Haeckel terms his opponents "a howling
pack."

† Huxley's *American Addresses*, p. 148.

‡ Büchner's *Force and Matter*, Preface, p. 86.

arrogance in the darkest ages of Papal superstition surpassing, or perhaps equalling, the arrogance displayed in the utterances quoted above. *

The whole question, as Professor Max Müller justly asked, " Is it true ? " resolves itself into this—Is man's origin a separate act of creative power on the part of an Omnipotent Being whom we call God, as revealed in His word, or has man been evolved through an infinite cycle of ages, either from a monkey and an ascidian tadpole, according to Darwin ?—or from the " sand-eel," in which Professor Haeckel thinks he has discovered the *missing link* between man and beast ?—or from that still more original particle of inorganic matter called *monera, i.e.,* the primeval atom of protoplasm, according to the theory of Professor Huxley ?—or from that of Professor Oken, the plagiarist of Lucretius, as

* See a Layman's protest in the *Contemporary Review* of April, 1881, entitled, " The Arrogance of Modern Scepticism."

he was of Democritus, who lived in the
4th century B.C., who traced back every
living creature and every thing without
life to *nothing ?*

You have hitherto heard what Mr. Darwin 'and some of his friends have to say
for themselves on behalf of the Evolution
theory of man's descent from a tadpole, or
from less than nothing; I propose to reverse the picture, and consider what the
most eminent scientists of the 19th century
have said on the same subject.

MEN OF SCIENCE OF THE 19TH CENTURY.

1. I propose to begin this list with one
of the most distinguished names on the
roll of science of that period, and whom
you may regard as the firm friend rather
than the opponent of the Darwinian philosophy. I refer to the well-known Professor TYNDALL, who in his Address at
Liverpool before the British Association
in 1870, together with that at Norwich in
1868, *On the Use and Limit of the Imagination
in Science,* and also with that delivered

as President of the British Association at Belfast in 1874, frankly and fully explains his views on the chief doctrine of Darwinism as it stood towards the close of the 19th century. From these Addresses I propose to make some extracts, by which you may clearly understand his thoughts on the subject, proceeding on the principle manifested by King Agrippa when he said to the Apostle Paul, "Thou art permitted to speak for thyself."

"I do not," says Professor Tyndall, "think this Evolution hypothesis is to be flouted away contemptuously: I do not think it is to be denounced as wicked. It is to be brought before the bar of disciplined reason, and there justified or condemned. Fear not the Evolution hypothesis. Steady yourselves in its presence upon that faith in the ultimate triumph of truth which was expressed by old Gamaliel, when he said—'If it be of God, ye cannot overthrow it; if it be of man, it will come to nought.' Under the fierce light of scientific enquiry, *this hypothesis is sure to be dissipated if it possess not a core of truth.* Trust me, its existence as an hypothesis in the mind is quite compatible with the simultaneous existence of all those virtues to which the term Christian has been applied. It does not solve—it does not profess to solve—the ultimate mystery of this universe. It leaves, in fact, that mystery untouched. For *granting the nebula and its potential life*, the question whence came they? would still remain to baffle and bewilder us. At bottom the hypothesis does nothing more than 'transport the conception of life's origin to an indefinitely distant past.' " *

With the exception of " granting the potential life of the nebula," most cultured Christians would agree with the extract given above. But this claim for the nebula possessing " potential life " is even stronger than Mr. Darwin's " if." It contains the whole gist of the difference

---

* *Use and Limit of the Imagination in Science*, p. 49.

between the believer in the God of the Bible and the speculating materialist. It can never be conceded by the one; it never will be given up, I presume, by the other.

Again, Professor Tyndall, while justly making on behalf of science "claims for the unrestricted right of search," observes—"It is not to the point to say that the views of Darwin and Spencer may be wrong. Here I should agree with you, deeming it indeed *certain that these views will undergo modification......* The world embraces not only a Newton, but a Shakespeare *—not only a Darwin, but a Carlyle (though the latter has pronounced the theory of the former to be '*deluded insanity*'). Not in each of these, but in all, is human nature whole. They are not opposed, but supplementary—not mutually exclusive, but *reconcilable !* And if, unsatisfied with them all, the human mind, with the yearning of a pilgrim

---

* See Appendix M.

for his distant home, will still turn to the Mystery from which it has emerged, seeking so to fashion it as to give unity to thought and faith......casting aside all the restrictions of *Materialism,* I would affirm this to be a field for the noblest exercise of what, in contrast with the *knowing* faculties, may be called *the creative faculties of man.* Here, however, I touch a theme too great for me to handle, but which will assuredly be handled by the loftiest minds when you and I, like streaks of morning cloud, shall have melted into the infinite azure of the past."* " The *creative* faculties of man ! " Is not this sailing very close *to,* and very fast *with,* a wind which blows from a very strong *Materialistic* quarter ?

But it is somewhat difficult to understand Tyndall's meaning, when he uses the words " Matter " and " Materialism." If he means, as Goethe used the term, to define " the living garment of God," it is beauti-

---

* Tyndall's *Belfast Address,* p. 65.

ful, though not correct, for the ordinary use of the term is what is called " brute matter," but his words seem to imply something distinct and apart from God.   And thus, in his *Belfast Address*, while noticing the theory of Epicurus, and Lucretius, whose god appears to have been the " fortuitous concourse of atoms," and pointing out that " Mr. Darwin does not say how his one primordial form has been introduced," Professor Tyndall declares how " Molecular force becomes structural," and that " it requires no great boldness of thought to extend its play into organic nature, and to recognize in molecular force the agency by which both plants and animals are built up. . . . Divorced from matter, where is life to be found ? Whatever our *faith* may say, our *knowledge* shows them to be indissolubly joined.   Every meal we eat, and every cup we drink, illustrates the mysterious control of Mind by Matter. . . . . Is there not a temptation to close to some extent with Lucretius, when he affirms that ' Nature is seen to do all things spontaneously of herself, without the meddling of the gods ? '—or with Bruno, when he declares ' Matter to be the universal mother, who brings forth all things as the fruit of her own womb ? ' . . . . By an intellectual necessity I cross the boundary of the experimental evidence, and *discern in Matter the promise and potency of all terrestrial life*." *

I think it is evident from these passages, if Professor Tyndall considers that Darwin's hypothesis respecting Evolution will inevitably undergo modification, he assumes Matter to be a sort of Deity possessed with the power of creating life. Hence he concludes that " not alone the more ignoble forms of animal life—not alone the noble forms of the horse and lion—not alone the exquisite and wonderful mechanism of the human body, but the human mind itself—emotion, intellect, will, and all their phenomena, were once latent in a fiery cloud. . . . At the present moment all

* *Belfast Address*, pp. 53—55.

our philosophy, poetry, science and art—
Plato, Shakespeare, Newton and Raphael—
are potential in the fires of the sun." *

2. Let me quote the testimony of a very
distinguished foreigner, Professor Agassiz,
whose scientific knowledge was such that
he was as able to give an authoritative
opinion of the "Evolution theory" as
any man of modern times. I have already
noticed what he says of the *Transmutation
theory*, viz., that "it was wholly without
foundation in fact." And again, in his
Comparative Anatomy, he plainly contradicts the Darwinian theory. "Man," he
says, does *not* descend from the mammals
which preceded him into the *tertiary* age."

3. In the same way Professor Sir
Richard Owen, of the very highest au-
thority in such matters, contradicts the
Darwinian hypothesis by declaring that

* *Scientific Use of the Imagination*, p. 47. See an
excellent article in *Blackwood's Magazine*, November,
1874, on "Modern Scientific Materialism." Also
another on Professor Tyndall's teaching in the same
magazine of July, 1871.

" the embryo of man does *not* pass through the lower forms of animals." And again, he teaches that " observation of the actual change of any one species into another has *not yet* been recorded." And so in his *Classification of Animals*, Owen again affirms that—" Man is the sole species of his genus, and the sole representative of his order and sub-class." Adding, with the confidence of a master-mind, " Thus, I trust, has been furnished *the confutation of the notion of a transformation of the ape into man* " (p. 103).

4. Professor MAX MULLER, as before noticed, deems it " the duty of every friend of truth to resist with all his might the hasty conclusions of the Darwinian school."

5. Professor CLERK MAXWELL asserts that "No theory of Evolution can be formed to account for the similarity of molecules. Science is incompetent to reason on creation of matter itself *out of nothing*."

6. Professor PHILLIPS, as already noticed, teaches that " No one advanced in philo-

sophy will ever be satisfied with laws which had no author, works which had no maker, and co-ordinations which had no designer."

7. Professor MAIN, of Oxford, says—"In accepting *the Biblical narrative of man's creation*, we need not repudiate one fact accurately deduced from modern scientific research."

8. Professor CHALLIS, of Cambridge, confirms his brother-professor's opinion, by observing that "The language of Scripture neither is nor can be contrary to the language of Science."

9. Professor STOKES, Secretary of the Royal Society, in his Address as President of the British Association in 1869, when speaking of the organic structures of life, says—"Let us fearlessly trace the dependance of link upon link, as far as it may be given us to trace it, but let us take heed that in thus studying second causes, we forget not the First Cause, nor shut our eyes to the wonderful *proofs of design*, which, in the

study of beings especially, meet us at every step."

10. Professor PRITCHARD, in his address at the Brighton Congress of 1874, in speaking of the irresistible proofs from teleology, which satisfied the minds of such reasoners as PALEY and BUTLER, CHALMERS and WHEWELL, that He who " planted the ear " and He who " made the eye," to use the language of the Psalmist, was an Almighty Designer and Creator, observes that this argument, which may be well termed unanswerable, " has carried conviction, from the time of Socrates to that of Cuvier, to the foremost minds of the human race, and found almost its sole antagonists among *spinners of cobwebs and dreamers of dreams.* . . . The prints of Divine forethought, and the convictions they engender, are scattered over the face of universal nature, and ploughed into the very subsoil of the human mind." Hence, he adds, " No chemist, with all his wonderful art, has ever yet witnessed the evolution of a living thing from those lifeless molecules of matter and force."

11. Professor TAIT, in his *Recent Researches in Physical Science*, combats the speculations of Darwin, who "tells us that even for a comparatively brief portion of recent geological history, three hundred millions of years will not suffice" to enable him to discover the missing link, which he thinks might easily be found, were it not for what he considers "the imperfection of the geological record." Hence Professor TAIT points out that "The Law of the Dissipation of Energy, discovered by Sir W. THOMSON, enables us distinctly to say that the present order of things *has not been evolved* through infinite past time by the agency of laws now at work, but must have had a distinct beginning. . . . Ten millions of years is *the utmost* we can give to geologists for their speculations as to the history of the lowest orders of fossils, and for all the changes that have taken place on the earth's surface since vegetable life of the lowest known form was capable of existing there."

12. Professor Lionel Beale, in his *Life Theories and Religious Thought*, combats the opinion entertained by many Darwinians, that the doctrine of man's descent from the lower animals is not contradicted by the Mosaic record, which makes man a separate act of creative power; and asserts that the "part of Darwinism which includes the evolution of living beings by physical laws is *utterly opposed to every principle of religion*." This has been confirmed by Dr. Parker, President of the Microscopical Society, in a very conclusive way. At one time he was engaged with Professor Huxley in making experiments at the South Kensington Museum, in order to prove if possible the connection between man and the rest of creation; the result of which was, as he told Capt Petrie, the Secretary of the Victoria Institute, " there was no point at which they appeared to join; " adding, " there is such an immeasurable gulf between man, with all his attributes, and the rest of creation; and *every thing*

tends to prove that he must have been a separate creation."

13. In reply to some of Mr. Darwin's candid avowals—*e.g.*, when he says, " To suppose that the eye could have been formed by NATURAL SELECTION seems absurd in the highest possible degree ; "† and again when he writes, " The chief cause of our natural unwillingness to admit that *one species has given birth to other and distinct species*, is that we are always slow in admitting any great change of which we do not see the intermediate steps "‡—without dwelling upon the fact that all observation, all experiments and all experience are against such . a theory—it will be sufficient to remember the wise teaching of one of the master- minds of the 19th century, Professor SEDGEWICK, of Cambridge, who, in his *Discourse on the Studies of the University*, justly points out that " Analysis consists

---

* *Transactions of the Victoria Institute*, vol. vii., p. 282.
† *Origin of Species*, p. 186.   ‡ Ibid., p. 481.

in making experiments and observations, and in drawing general conclusions from them by induction, and admitting of no objections against the conclusions but such as are taken from experiments or other certain truths; for *hypotheses are not to be regarded in experimental philosophy*." And Mr. Darwin, at the close of his life, frankly admitted that his Evolution theory was "only an hypothesis."*

14. Hence Professor GOODSIR, of Edinburg, one of the foremost men of his age, justly asserted that "man is entirely separated from animals by reason of his spiritual nature *standing alone in the great work of creation;* as it is in virtue of his possession of a spiritual principle, by which alone he is capable of thought and speech, and is impressed with the belief of moral truth and divine agency, that man stands alone among the organized beings of the globe."†

---

* See Preface.

† Goodsir's *Anatomical Memoirs*, i., p. 271.

15. With the Scotch professor agrees his distinguished brother from the Emerald Isle, Professor PORTER, of Belfast, who justly observes, " Science shows that life is an entity, a power, apart from and above matter, but that in its essence it eludes the keen eye of the philosopher. The whole teachings of science are, so far as they can go, in harmony with that simple but sublime record, ' And the Lord God formed man of the dust of the ground, and breathed into his nostrils the breath of life; and man became a living soul.' " *

16. Professor St. GEORGE MIVART, a learned member of the Church of Rome, and author of so able a work on *The Genesis of Species*, that it was commonly said at the time, " Darwinism has received a blow from which it will never recover," —in his *Lessons from Nature*, says he had two main objects in view in writing the *Genesis* : " † 1st, to show that the Darwinian

* Porter's Lecture on *Science and Revelation*, p. 19.
† Compare the object which Darwin had in view in his *Origin of Species*. See p. 116 of this work.

theory is untenable, and that 'Natural Selection' is not *the* origin of species; 2nd, to demonstrate that nothing even in Mr. Darwin's theory, and *à fortiori* nothing in Evolution generally, was necessarily antagonistic to Christianity"(p. 429). Hence he concludes in another of his works, entitled *Man and Apes*, in which he pronounces Darwinism to be "*a crude and untenable hypothesis*," that "If it be true that the long-lost structural character of certain apes is due to 'Atavism' and 'Reversion,' in their modern descendants, which formerly existed in hypothetical ancestors; and that man and monkey are diverging descendants of a creature with certain cerebral characters, then that remote ancestor must also have had—

1. The *wrist* of the chimpanzee; 2. The *voice* of a long-armed ape; 3. The *ear* of the gorilla; 4. The *nose* of the long-tailed proboscis monkey; 5. The *chin* of the siamang; 6. The *skull* of an American ape; 7. The *ischium* of a slender loris; 8. The *whiskers* and *beard* of a sakis;

9. The *liver and stomach* of the *sibbong ;* and a *number of other things*, in which the various several forms of higher or lower primates respectively approximate to man " (pp. 152, 177).

Such was the interesting creature from whom Darwin and his numerous disciples suppose themselves to have sprung ; and of whom the master says especially that there is " no reason " why you should be " ashamed " of having such a distinguished progenitor, though others may differ from him on this point in accordance with the aphorism of Terence—" *Quot homines, tot sententiæ : suus cuique mos.*"

17. The last member of the professorial class, whom I shall have the honour of quoting as to his opinion on the Darwinian philosophy, is one of the greatest names in the long roll of celebrities of the 19th century, Dr. VIRCHOW, Professor of Pathology in the University of Berlin, and by general consent master of the science he professes, delivered a brilliant address at the Munich Conference of

German Naturalists, September, 1878, which was subsequently published with the title of *The Freedom of Science in the Modern State*. The address forms a remarkable exception to the bold assumption of the Darwinians, that mankind has come to the front through endless changes from lower to higher forms of life. The address is a most impressive protest in the name and interest of true science against that pseudo-scientific dogmatism which first propounds unverified speculations as the conclusions of science, and then reiterates them in the circle of admiring disciples as infallibly true, till their universal acceptance is boldly assumed, and all who doubt their crude assumptions are branded, to use the coarse words of Louis Büchner, as "mental slaves," "speculative idiots," "yelping curs," &c. In reply to this specimen of Atheistic folly, Professor Virchow justly points out that "every positive progress in the region of prehistoric anthropology has removed further the theory that whenever a skull was found in a peat bog, or in pile dwellings, or in ancient caves, people fancied they saw in it a wonderful token of an inferior being, still quite undeveloped. They smelt out the very scent of the ape. Yet when we study the fossil man of the quaternary period, we always find a MAN just such as men are now."

In reply to the demand of Haeckel and other infidels, that the Evolution theory should form a part of universal primary education in Germany, Professor Virchow observes : "When Herr Haeckel says that it is a question for the educator whether the theory of human evolution should be at once laid down as the basis of education, and the 'protoplastic soul' be assumed as the foundation of all ideas concerning spiritual being, and whether the teaching is to trace back the origin of the human race to the lowest classes of the organic kingdom—nay, still further, to *spontaneous generation*—this is, in my opinion, *a perversion of the teacher's office.* If the Evolution theory be as certain as Herr

M

Haeckel assumes it to be, then we must demand, then it is a necessary claim, that it should be introduced into the schools."

Further, in reply to the theory that the human soul was nothing but " CARBON," with a flavour of phosphorus,* and that as Haeckel explained the development of all existing organisms from a single organic cell called "*Protoplasm*," Dr. Virchow, while admitting the *possibility* of the long vainly-sought-for missing link between man and beast being discovered, " if not," as he says, " with the apes, yet perhaps, as Herr Voght now supposes, at some other point,"— quietly adds :—

" I freely acknowledge that this is a *desideratum* in science. I should not be surprised if such a proof were produced ; *but it has not been done as yet.* You are aware that I am now specially engaged in the study of ANTHROPOLOGY; but I am

* It was a dictum ascribed to the German Moles-chott, "Ohne Phosphor kein Gedanke."

bound to declare that every positive advance which we have made in the person of prehistoric anthropology has *actually removed us further from the proof of such a connexion.* As a matter of fact, we must positively recognise that *as yet* there always exists a sharp line of demarcation between man and the ape. *We cannot teach, we cannot pronounce it to be a conquest of science, that man descends from the ape or any other animal.* We can *only* indicate it as *an hypothesis.* From the repeated experience of the past we ought to take a *signal warning,* lest we should unnecessarily impose on ourselves the obligation, or succumb to the temptation to draw conclusions at a time when we are not justified in so doing." And he adds this just remark, which might well induce caution to all sceptics, even to those who have gone the lengths of Professors Haeckel or Huxley—"Whosoever speaks or writes for the public is bound to examine with double care how much of that which he knows and says is objectively true. With perfect truth Bacon declared, 'Knowledge is power,' but also defined that knowledge, which meant, not speculative, nor unproved theories, but what was objective and actual and true."

You have thus the testimony of twenty learned PROFESSORS of the 19th century respecting the *Evolution theory ;* and you will have seen how every one of them (save Professor Tyndall, who rightly judged that it would be modified by time) condemned it with more or less vigour; and you who live in these more enlightened days, will naturally wonder how such an "unverified theoretic conception" could have bewitched the minds of any but those who allow imagination to get the better of their reason.

I might add to the above catena an infinite number of other celebrities of the same age, such as Murchison, Lyell, Humboldt, Principal Dawson, Joachim, Barrante, Dugald Stewart, Dr. Hunt of the Anthropological Society, Carlyle, the great statesmen of the 19th century, such as Lord Beaconsfield and Mr. Gladstone, &c., &c., all of whom have rejected such a fanciful theory as that man has been developed from a tadpole, or · sinking deeper in the slough of Materialistic error, from an atom of lifeless protoplasm!

I will, however, content myself with adding the testimony of three more celebrities, who, though not bearing the honourable title of "Professors," have proved themselves to be fully qualified to deliver an authoritative opinion on this momentous question.

1. The first witness I shall call is a very distinguished member of the French Institute, the most scientific society in the world, which thrice rejected Mr. Darwin's claim of membership on account of the unscientific nature of his theories. In M. A. DE QUATREFAGES, you have an authority on this special question who has perhaps as good claims for being heard as any which England can produce; and this

is what he says about the Evolution theory of Mr. Darwin:—

"It is evident, especially after the most ·fundamental principles of Darwinism, that an organised being cannot be a descendant of another whose development is an inverse order to its own. Consequently, in accordance with these principles, *man cannot be considered as the descendant of any simian type whatever.*"*

2. My second witness shall be that famous Naturalist, FRANK BUCKLAND, the greater son of a great father, whose authority on all subjects connected with the fishy tribe was of a higher nature than that of Darwin himself. Two days before his lamented death in 1880, he completed the Preface to his latest work, *The Natural History of British Fishes.* With fidelity to his Creator, as well as to the fame of his earthly father, himself a

---

* *The Human Species.* By A. De Quatrefages, Membre de l'Institut (Académie des Sciences), and Foreign Member of the Royal Society. International Scientific Series, vol. **xxvi.**, p. 111.

dying man on the verge of eternity, he
made the following declaration of his scientific creed respecting EVOLUTION in these
telling words :—

"I have another object in writing
this book: it is to endeavour to show
the truth of the good old doctrines of
the 'Bridgewater Treatises,' which have
so ably demonstrated ' the power, wisdom
and goodness of God as manifested in
creation.' Of late years, the doctrines
of so-called EVOLUTION and DEVELOPMENT
have seemingly gained ground amongst
those interested in Natural History; but I
have too much faith in the good sense and
natural acumen of my countrymen to
think *these tenets will be very long-lived.* To
put matters very straight, I steadfastly
believe that the great Creator, as indeed
we are directly told, made all things
perfect and ' very good ' from the beginning; perfect and very good is every
thing now found to be, and will continue so
to the end of time."

You know, my scientific friends of the

21st century, how truly Frank Buckland's anticipations have come to pass, how 'short-lived' was the queer delusion of man's descent from an ascidian tadpole; still shorter the Atheistic doctrine of man having been developed from dead matter, such as a piece of carbon, by the process of spontaneous generation; and now you naturally look back with wonder and amazement at the wild speculations of the Darwinites two centuries ago, when you see that the Evolution theory has tumbled to pieces like a pack of cards, or, using the more poetic language of Professor Tyndall, that it has quite "melted away into the infinite azure of the past."

My third witness is the Rev. F. O. MORRIS, Rector of Nunburnholme, in Yorkshire, whose *History of British Birds* constitutes him as distinguished an authority in the feathery tribe as Frank Buckland was in that of fishes. Mr. Morris' opinion appears in a correspondence which he once had with the editor of the *Guardian* newspaper, and though expressed in terms unnecessarily strong for the occasion, are very valuable as showing what a learned Naturalist of the 19th century thought of Darwinism and its numerous disciples. He thus delivers his testimony :—

"In one of Miss Edgeworth's tales she describes the 'ineffable contempt and indignation' with which Sir Plantagenet Mowbray received the proposition of Marvel, the Lincolnshire farmer, to purchase his heronry near Spalding. 'Ineffable contempt and indignation' is the only feeling which any one of common sense and of a right mind must feel at the astounding puerilities of Darwinism, its ten thousand times worse than childish absurdities, contempt for them in themselves, and indignation at the criminal injury which the miserable infidelity of the wretched system has done to the minds of too many."

Lamenting the unseemly strength of Mr. Morris' language, it nevertheless faithfully exhibits the feelings which the

most thoughtful *savans* of the 19th century,
who still accepted Scripture as the only
infallible guide, entertained for what I
hope I shall not be deemed wanting in
courtesy to the illustrious founder of
the theory, if I am constrained to term it
THE DARWINIAN CRAZE.

But inasmuch as there were a few very
learned men of that age who believed, or
supposed that they believed in Darwinism,
it will be but fair if I quote some of them,
in order to show you what was said at the
time on the other side of the question.

MR. DARWIN'S DISCIPLES.

Here Professor Huxley has the first
claim on your attention, not only on account of his talents, which are undoubtedly
of the highest order, but also for the
boundless admiration which he entertained
when living for the master and founder of
the school, whom he compares to Aristotle
among the ancients, and to Sir Isaac
Newton amongst the moderns.

Lamenting the strength of the language

which he occasionally employed against
the ministers of religion, when it was
evident that he had got out of his depth,
I would invite your attention to three
branches of the Darwinian theory with
which the name of Professor Huxley was
more or less identified, which may be
enumerated as follows :—

1. Concerning the Origin of Species.
2. Concerning the Antiquity of Man.
3. Concerning the Unity of Race.

I must begin by warning you that this
learned professor went far ahead of the
illustrious Darwin in his range of free
thought; as we may judge from the
answer which he once gave to Professor
Mivart in reply to his very natural remark
that "without a belief in a personal God
there was no religion worthy of the
name:" to which Huxley thus replied—
" This is a matter of opinion. But it may
be asserted, with less reason to fear contradiction (?), that the worship of a personal
God, who, on Mr. Mivart's hypothesis,

must have used language studiously calculated to deceive His creatures and worshippers, is no religion worthy of the name."*

An eminent German scholar of the highest fame in that age, the illustrious Niebuhr, takes an entirely different view from that of Professor Huxley, as he once justly wrote to a friend, and you may be sure that every one who has the slightest and most elementary knowledge . of the Gospel will agree with him—"Christianity without a personal God is no Christianity at all to me, though it may be a very ingenious philosophy. I have often said I do not know what to do with a metaphysical God, and that I will have none but the God of the Bible, who is heart to heart with us." †

Professor Huxley offers, however, a very good answer to himself by a remark which he makes in his *Life of Hume,*

---

* Huxley, in *Contemporary Review*, Nov. 1871, p. 458.
† Niebuhr's *Life and Letters*, vol. ii., p. 123.

saying—"All science starts with hypotheses—in other words, with assumptions
that are unproved, while they may be and
often are erroneous" (p. 55). Now this
was exactly the position of the Darwinian
philosophy at the close of the 19th century,
after 100 years' trial. Started originally
by Lord Monboddo towards the end of the
18th century, it remained in its cradle,
overwhelmed with the swaddling clothes
which Mr. Darwin's disciples heaped upon
the unhappy babe during a century of
almost unequalled progress in scientific
discovery, until the year before his death
in 1882, Mr. Darwin acknowledged to
a friendly enquirer that his Evolution
theory was "only an hypothesis" still.
You, therefore, Gentlemen, living in this
more enlightened age of the 21st century,
when the theory has melted away and
evaporated, like so many other unsubstantial theories, "into the infinite azure
of the past," will naturally wonder that
your ancestors two centuries ago should
have been so "bewitched," as they

undoubtedly were, by the "hypothesis" of Darwin, and the bolder speculations of his learned disciple, Professor Huxley. Your wonder will be still more excited when you hear that at one of the Church Congresses (Reading, 1883) of that time, Professor Fowler had the temerity to declare, on the principle I suppose that—

"Fools rush in where angels fear to tread "—

that " Evolution was a certainty ; that man was evolved like other animals ; and that special creation of known forms could not be admitted." You can afford to smile at such a whimsical display of ignorance peculiar to the close of the 19th century.

Professor Fowler, however, had a congenial supporter in Professor Huxley, who at that time declared that " *Origin of Species* has worked as complete a revolution in biological science as the *Principia* (of Newton) did in astronomy "! This wild assumption, which the testimony of the last two centuries has so completely overthrown, may remind you of the conduct of certain Jesuits, when publishing an edition of Newton's *Principia*, they were compelled in the interests of the Church of Rome to prefix to their edition the following cautious avowal—

"Newton, in his third book, adopts the hypothesis of the earth's motion. And we are unable to explain his propositions without admitting the same hypothesis. Hence we are compelled to assume a character different from our own, for we profess obedience to the decrees promulgated by the Pope against the motion of the earth"!!!*

Remarkable instance of blind obedience to the great "false prophet" of the age, as the Book of Revelation terms the head of the Roman Church, under the name of Babylon the Great, the Mother of harlots, for which certain professing members of the Church of England, like Dr. F. G. Lee of Lambeth, were once so eagerly panting,

* Preface to Newton's *Principia*, edited by the Jesuits Le Suer and Jacquier, 1823.

as it accords so perfectly with the principles of Romanism, in its most true and ultra
form, as expressed by the founder of the
Jesuits in his famous aphorism, "What I
see *white* I believe to be black, if the
Church of Rome so define it to be." *

I cannot think that Professor Huxley
seriously meant to assert that Darwin's
"hypothesis" of all mankind having originally been evolved from the larvæ of
an ascidian tadpole, or according to his
own expressed view of the Evolution
theory, going some steps further back into
chaos, from an atom of lifeless protoplasm,
is to be for a moment compared in point of
truth with what the Jesuits of Rome are
pleased to term, "Newton's hypothesis
of the earth's motion." If he did, it affords
another proof of the wisdom of Mr. Gladstone's remark—"I have always thought,"
he once said, "that scientific men run too
much in a groove.   They do noble work in

---

* *Exercises of St. Ignatius Loyola*, edited by the
late Cardinal Wiseman.

their own special lines of study and research, but they are too often indisposed
to give any attention whatever to matters
which seem to conflict with their established modes of thought. Indeed, they not
unfrequently attempt to deny that into
which they have never enquired, not
sufficiently realizing the fact that there
may possibly be forces in nature of which
they know nothing." *

In place of finding a parallel between
Newton and Darwin, Professor Huxley
might, I think, have found a more appro-
priate parallel for the latter in the teaching of one Voetius, an old Dutch divine
of the 17th century, which he states as
follows :—"We affirm that the sun flies
round the earth every 24 hours, and that
the earth rests immovable in the centre of
the universe, with all divines, natural
philosophers and astronomers, Jews and

---

* See a periodical called *Light*, of Nov. 8th, 1884,
with an account of "Mr. Gladstone at a Seance"
on the preceding Oct. 29th.

Mohammedans, Greeks and Latins, excepting one or two of the ancients and the modern followers of Copernicus."

It is difficult to suppose that Professor Huxley could really believe that the educated clergy of the 19th century taught such stuff as Voetius credited all the *savans* with two hundred years before; yet if words have any definite meaning, certainly the learned professor, in his address to the clergy at Sion College, Nov. 21st, 1867, seems to imply as much, as his words can scarcely bear any other meaning.

"You tell your congregations," said he, "that the world was made 6000 years ago in the period of six days. Thus you hold and teach that men of science like myself are liable to pains and penalties, as men who are guilty of breaking or disputing great moral laws. I am bound to say I do not believe these statements you make and teach, and I am further bound to say that I do not and cannot call to mind amongst the thoughtful men of science and research, one who believes these things; but, on the other hand, who do not believe the exact contrary."

It is not necessary to point out to you in this age the marvellous delusion under which Professor Huxley was labouring when he lectured the clergy at Sion College; and which delusion he subsequently attempted to defend in his *Lay Sermons*, by declaring that the orthodox doctrine, or, as he termed it, " the Catholic doctrine, was this—that the work of creation took place in the space of six natural days "— adding, " that the universe was created in six natural days is hopelessly inconsistent with the doctrine of Evolution " (p. 452); to which he might have added with far greater approximation to the truth, " that the universe was created in six natural days is hopelessly inconsistent with the infallible Word of Truth, as recorded by Moses, in the book of Genesis." If Professor Huxley, with all his learning, had but the faintest conception of the elements of the Hebrew language in which Moses wrote the first five books of Scripture, he would never have committed the unpardonable blunder of supposing the Bible taught that the universe was created by Almighty God in six natural days!!! What the Bible really does teach is simply this—that "In the beginning of eternity, when the Word was God, God called into existence, or created the essence of the heavens and the essence of the earth—*i.e.*, the whole universe." And after these had done their part, if I may use such a term, in the course, it may have been, of millions of years, the Almighty thought fit to prepare earth for the habitation of those created beings, whom He made after His own image and likeness, or as it is tersely rendered in our English version, "In six days the Lord made heaven and earth." But no competent scholar would *make* the mistake which Professor Huxley did at Sion College, of confounding the two Hebrew words translated "created" and "made" as bearing the same meaning!

Had Professor Huxley attacked the philosophers of the 17th century in this manner, in place of the clergy of the 19th, he would have been far nearer the truth than he was when he delivered his address at Sion College in the year 1867; for Lecky, in his instructive work on the *History of the Rise and Influence of the Spirit of Rationalism in Europe*, relates that "According to the great philosophers of the 17th century, our world was a vast and complicated mechanism *called into existence and elaborated instantaneously in all its parts by the creative fiat of the Deity*" (vol. i., p. 315).

Moreover, Professor Huxley ought to have known that Bacon, the prince of lay philosophers (who, as Lecky points out, "notwithstanding his great genius, was totally unable to grasp the discoveries of Copernicus, Galileo, Tycho Brahè, Kepler and Gilbert"), rejected the greatest discovery of the age in the Copernican system; and possibly the professor may not have been aware that Copernicus was numbered amongst that class which he appears so heartily to despise—viz., *the* *clergy*. Hence, he should have confined his censures at all events to the Roman priests of the 16th, and not to the Protestant clergy of the 19th century, for as soon as the grand discovery of Copernicus began to circulate amongst the literati of Europe, the suspicions of the Roman theologians were aroused, and the opinion of the earth's motion was authoritatively censured; first of all in the person of Copernicus, who was accused by the Cardinals of the Congregation of the Index of teaching the Pythagorean doctrine respecting the earth's motion and the immobility of the sun; and seventeen years later, "in the condemnation, the imprisonment, and perhaps the torture of Galileo." *

About two years after the episode at Sion College, I find the same learned professor replying to a courteous invitation of the Committee of the Dialectical Society of June 29th, 1869, who were seeking to induce men of science to investigate the

---

* See Appendix N.

claims of "Spiritualism," in the following characteristic language—" If anybody could endow me with the faculty of *listening to the chatter of old women and curates in the nearest cathedral town,* I should decline the privilege, having better things to do." *

In one of his "Lay Sermons," Professor Huxley adopts a similar tone towards all who decline to accept the Darwinian teaching as "infallible" as that of the Pope of Rome. "Everybody has read Mr. Darwin's book on the *Origin of Species,* or at least has given an opinion upon its merits or demerits; pietists, whether lay or ecclesiastic, decry it with the mild railing† which sounds so charitable; bigots denounce it with ignorant invective; old ladies of both sexes consider it decidedly a dangerous book; and even *savans,* which have no better mud to throw, quote antiquated writers to show that its author is no better than an ape himself; while

---

* See Appendix O.   † See Appendix P.

every philosophical thinker hails it (Darwin's *Origin of Species*) *as a veritable Whitworth gun in the armory of liberation*" (p. 280).

Surely Professor Huxley ought to have allowed that there had been some eminent men of science, such as Sir Richard Owen, or Agassiz, or Virchow, *cum multis aliis*, who were deserving the name of "Philosophers," but who were never able to accept the fabulous theory of Darwinism.

The learned professor explained his theory of the *Origin of Species* in the following manner:—"If a drop of blood be drawn from the finger, there will be seen a small number of colourless corpuscules, which exhibit at once a marvellous activity. The substance thus active is a mass of *protoplasm*, and its activity differs in detail rather than in principle from that of the protoplasm of the nettle. Under sundry circumstances the corpuscule dies, and becomes distended into a round mass, in the midst of which is seen a smaller spherical body, called its *nucleus*. In the earliest condition of the

human organism, it is nothing but an
aggregation of such corpuscules. And
thus a nucleated mass of protoplasm turns
out to be what may be termed the
structural unit of the human body. As a
matter of fact, the body in its earliest state
is a mere multiple of such units; and in
its perfect condition, it is a multiple of
such units variously modified." *

All these nebulous utterances, when.
divested of scientific entanglements, may
be understood to mean, that by eating
mutton, to use the professor's words,
" sheep is transubstantiated into man."
Or if you reverse the process, you have
professorial authority for assuming that
by feeding on eagles you ought to be able
to fly; or that parrots would make as
good after-dinner speeches in articulate
language as Huxley himself did in 1871,
when at the Royal Academy dinner he
told the company that " parrots often
talked what deserves the name of sense, as

* Huxley's *Lay Sermons*, pp. 140, 152.

much as a great deal which it would be rude to call nonsense,"—a remark in the professor's usually cynical and caustic language, which reminds one of the very learned parrot mentioned by Darwin as "the sole living creature which could speak the language of a lost tribe"! Darwin's bird, however, scarcely equals in point of intelligence another parrot of the Roman Catholic persuasion according to the *Glories of Mary*, a work which was much in use amongst the Papists of the 19th century, where you will find at p. 67 the following idle legend related, and inasmuch as the work is highly commended by Cardinal Manning, we conclude it is accepted by the Church of Rome.

"A parrot was taught to say, 'Hail! Mary.' A hawk was on the point of seizing it, when the bird cried out, '*Hail! Mary*'! In an instant the hawk fell dead. God intended to show thereby that if even an irrational creature was preserved by calling on Mary, how much more would those who are prompt in calling upon her when assaulted by devils, be delivered from them " ! ! !

Professor Huxley's theory of the doctrine of Transubstantiation, or, as he words it, of "sheep being transubstantiated into man," may remind you of what one of your own poets, William Shakespeare, of Stratford-upon-Avon, as some thought, or to speak more correctly, what the illustrious author of *Hamlet* wrote on the same subject. "Your worm * is your only emperor for diet: we fat all creatures else to fat us, and we fat ourselves for maggots: your fat king and your lean beggar is but variable service, two dishes to one table; that's the end. A man may eat fish with the worm that hath eaten of a king, and eat of the fish that hath fed of that worm." †

There appears, however, to have been considerable difference between the teaching of Darwin and that of his chief

---

* See Appendix Q.

† *Hamlet*, act iv., scene 3, 1. 22.

disciple Huxley, on the subject of the
Origin of Species. Whereas the former is
content with tracing back man's primeval
ancestor to the larvæ of an ascidian
tadpole, technically called *tunicaræ*, or
"sea squirt," into which the Supreme
Creator originally breathed life ; the latter
traces the pedigree, not confining it to
animal, or even vegetable life, but far
beyond, even to the azoic period, when
there was no sign of life in the mineral
kingdom—when every thing was hidden
in the nucleated cell of an atom of protoplasm, as he once stated in an after-
dinner speech already alluded to, that
"the recent progress of biological speculation leads to the conclusion that the scale
of being may be thus stated—minerals,
plants, animals, man, which, startling as
the announcement may be, must now take
rank as a scientific truth." Hence the
dogma that the Origin of Life, as well as
of Species, must be looked for in the
mineral, as preceding the vegetable and
the animal in the Geological series.

Professor Huxley's theory of tracing back the Origin of Life to dead matter, has found a warm upholder in another professor of foreign birth, viz., Professor Haeckel, who must be regarded as the rival, and indeed opponent, rather than the disciple of Darwin; so wide was the gulf respecting the Origin of Life between these two. On the continent the theory went often by the name of "*Haeckelism*," because its votaries were conscious that Haeckel's Atheism had little in common with Darwin's Christianity; Professor Haeckel's doctrine on the Origin of Life and Species may be summarily described in his words as follows :—"After the dead matter of carbon had gone on for count-less ages evolving, it had at . length brought forth a living creature in the shape of a lowly *monera*, which originated about the beginning of the Laurentian period by means of *spontaneous generation*... Without any doubt a long series of extinct *worms* were our direct ancestors."* To

* See Appendix R.

this bold avowal of Materialistic Atheism in its most objectionable form, Professor Tholuck has wisely remarked—" If a man is a *Materialist*, we Germans think he is not educated." Possibly Professor Haeckel may have been closely studying " Shake-speare," when he delivered himself of such nonsense that "worms were our direct ancestors; " or have been supping off that historic worm mentioned in *Hamlet*, already referred to; and which I repeat for the fun of the thing, as the only possible solution of Haeckel's wild theory—" Your worm is your only emperor for diet: we fat all creatures else to fat us, and we fat ourselves for maggots."

Leaving Professor Haeckel in the midst of his materialistic slough, I return to Professor Huxley, and having considered his views as to the *Origin of Life*, I notice briefly what he says respecting the ANTIQUITY OF MAN. On this point the wildness of sceptics in general and Professor Huxley in particular, exceeds, if possible, their wild speculations respecting the human pedigree. All believers in Scripture know the creation of the earth took place " in the beginning," and how many millions of years ago that was, the little mind of finite man has not the faintest idea. Scripture is also clear that the human race was called into existence by the fiat of the Creator in round numbers about 6000 years ago, and there is no evidence of man's existence on earth at any earlier period. Indeed, the earliest *proof*, as distinct from speculation, of man's exis- tence is to be found in a tablet in the Ashmolean Museum at Oxford, which, according to the new tablet of Abydos, may be safely dated about B.C. 2200, or perhaps a century earlier, the date which Champolion, the illustrious founder of Egyptology, rightly assigned to the oldest monuments in the land of Ham. I am aware that in the 19th century many half- informed chronologers persistently de- clared that the era of Menes,* the first co-

---

* See Appendix S.

Ionizer or king of Egypt after the Noachian flood, must be reckoned about B.C. 5000, but this speculative idea arose from a complete misunderstanding of the national historian Manetho. Those who knew anything of Egyptology, and relied upon the truth of Scripture, found ample proof from the monuments and the papyri, that in place of Manetho giving 1500 years, as his followers say that he does, for the duration of the first six dynasties, the real period was not more than 355 years. To make a comparison with British history. We know from the incoming of the Saxons to the days of Alfred, the first sole monarch of England, embraces a period of about four centuries; but if our historians had given each of the dynasties of the Heptarchy a separate and continuous reckoning for the duration of their respective years, that period would have been prolonged to over 2000 years! Just so have many of your Egyptian chronologers mistaken or purposely manipulated the testimony of Manetho.

But the late Baron Bunsen, a volumi-
nous writer on Egyptian matters, in his
Egypt's Place in Universal History (vol.
v.), has done worse; for not only has he endeavoured to disparage Scripture chronology in every possible way, but has lauded
Manetho up to the skies, affirming that by
means of this heathen scribe he had learned
TRUTH! Thus he apostrophises him of
whose writings we have the merest
fragmentary notices, mentioned by a few
subsequent writers like Josephus, Afri-
canus, and Eusebius, the earliest of whom,
Josephus, notices him in these uncompli-
mentary terms—" Manetho tells arrant
lies." Nevertheless, Bunsen is so excited
on his behalf as to give utterance to the
following—

> " Manetho, give us your name!
> Grateful, I offer to thee whatever through thee
>   I have learnt;
> Truth have I sought at thy hand: truth have
>   I found by that aid."
>
> *Egypt's Place, &c.,* vol. ii., p. 392.

Hence Bunsen carries out his delusion

o

to the fullest extent by declaring that the
Egyptians were skilful potters about 20,000
years B.C.; while he modestly assures other
speculators of the same school who were
somewhat in advance of his calculations,
that there is no reason to believe that man
was a denizen of earth at any earlier
period. He arrives at this conclusion from
the fact of some pieces of pottery having
been found at a certain depth in the
alluvial mud of the Nile, which he calculated would require upwards of 20,000
years to reach, allowing the rate of
sinkage so much a century. But his estimate was speedily blown to the winds by
the fact of some of this Nile pottery being
found stamped with the *Grecian honey-
suckle*, which proved that it could not
be older than Alexander the Great's
conquest of Egypt, *i.e.*, *circa* 300 years
B.C. And as if further to expose the
rashness of making such calculations about
the age of man on earth, shortly after the
Bunsen incident in the Nile mud, the late
Sir Robert Stephenson, when engineering

in the neighbourhood of Damietta, discovered in the alluvial deposits of the Nile,
at a greater depth than in the previous
case, *a brick bearing upon it the stamp of
Mehemet Ali, the ruler of Egypt in the 19th
century,* A.D.* ! ! !

But Bunsen, though he was sanguine
about Egypt having produced a colony of
pottery men as early as 20,000 years
B.C., until the Mehemet Ali brick dispersed
his theory to the winds, was a very
modest computer of the age compared
with the wilder speculations of Professor
Huxley, as he declared there was no
"valid reason" for allowing man a higher
antiquity than B.C. 20,000. At which bolder
sceptics laughed him to scorn, as one and
all affirmed this was not near long enough
for the human pedigree since his ancestor
had divested himself of his caudal appendage, as he passed, according to
Mr. Darwin's theory, from an old-world
monkey into the stage of uncivilized man!

---

* *London Quarterly Review*, No. li., p. 240.

Hence we find, among multitudes of others equally in error, the following speculations respecting the supposed antiquity of man, in contrast to the unerring word of truth.

1. Moses gives man an antiquity of about 6,000 years; and no proof, nor a scintilla of evidence, has ever yet been produced to show that this is wrong.

2. The late Baron Bunsen allowed man an antiquity of about 22,000 years.

3. Mr. Jukes, an English Geologist, ditto of 100,000 years.

4. Professor Fühlroth of Germany, ditto of 200,000 years.

5. M. Chabas, a French Egyptologer, ditto of 300,000 years.

6. The Chronology of the Brahmins, ditto of 4,320,000 years.

7. Dr. Hunt, late President of the Anthropological Society, ditto of 9,000,000.

8. Mr. Wallace, the famous Naturalist, ditto of 1,000,000,000 years.

9. Prof. Waitz, ditto of 35,000,000,000 years.

10. Prof. Huxley, ditto of —— (?) years.

We are unable to give any definite number of years to Huxley's estimate for the antiquity of man, because in place of limiting himself to the comparatively modest calculation of Professor Waitz, who only demands 35,000 million years for man's age on earth, Professor Huxley, in his speech at the Norwich Meeting of the British Association, asked if the different types of certain skulls did not—

"Point to a vastly remote period of time? And if so, did it not throw back *the appearance of man upon the globe to an era immeasurably more remote than has ever yet been assigned to it by the boldest speculators?*" *

This seems to imply that if Professor Haeckel declares that the direct ancestors of man were certain "extinct worms," and Mr. Darwin teaches that the larvæ of the ascidian tadpole were the primeval parents of the old-world monkey, which gradually evolved learned professors such as Huxley

---

* See Appendix T.

or Waitz themselves, the estimate of the latter—say 35,000,000,000 years for the supposed antiquity of man—is not sufficient for the rapacious maw of the former! Such was the teaching of Professor Huxley in the 19th century, antagonistic to the plain statements of Moses respecting the age of man on earth.

A third opinion pronounced by the same learned professor was against *the Unity of the Human Race.* Although both Moses and the Apostle Paul, in his address to the learned Athenians, alike taught that mankind were sprung from a single pair, as the latter expresses it, "God hath made of one blood all nations of men to dwell on all the face of the earth," Huxley, in order to carry out his principles that "scepticism is the highest of duties; blind faith the one unpardonable sin—" * declared that " Five-sixths of the public are taught this Adamitic monoganism (viz., that all mankind are descended from Adam), as if it

---

* Huxley's *Lay Sermons,* p. 2.

were an established truth, and believe it; I
do not, and I am not acquainted with any
man of science who does."* Thus while
Professor Huxley considers the Evolution
Theory to be "an established truth," he
declares the Scripture doctrine, that all
mankind have sprung from Adam, to be
unworthy the attention of any man of
science, as he does not know a single
one who believes it ! ! !

Possibly Professor Huxley's acquaintance among the scientific world of the
19th century was limited; as certainly
some of that age did believe in the
Bible, as I shall mention two or three
who avowed it, and who were, I conclude, without the charmed circle of
Huxley's acquaintance. It is true that
the notorious infidel Voltaire—whose
claim to rank as a man of science may
be inferred from his statement that the
shells found on the summit of the Alpine

---

* Huxley in the *Fortnightly Review*—"On the
Methods and Results of Ethnology."

mountains reached that lofty region, having dropped from the pockets of the Crusaders on their return from the East! —agrees with your learned professor, as he says, "None but blind men can doubt that the whites, negroes, Albinos, Hottentots, Laplanders, Chinese, and Americans, *are entirely distinct races.*" But there are those, with far higher claims to rank as men of science, who take an entirely opposite view. I will mention three or four, who, I conclude, had not the honour of being known to Huxley.

(1.) The Duke of Argyll observed, "*The unity of mankind* is too deeply interwoven with the fundamental doctrines of Christianity, for us to make any distinction between them."

(2.) Sir Charles Lyell taught that, "The unity of race from a single pair, was a doctrine against which there appears to be no sound objection."

(3.) Professor Pritchard, whose celebrated work on *The Natural History of*

Man, caused Dr. Carpenter to describe him as "a physiologist among physiologists, and a scholar among scholars," declared, after a masterly review and analysis of the whole subject, as his matured opinion respecting "all the distinct tribes of sentient beings in the universe, that we are entitled to draw confidently the conclusion that *all human races are of one species and one family.*"

(4.) Lastly, we have the testimony of Mr. Darwin himself, who declared in his work on *The Expression of the Emotions in Man and other Animals*,* to this effect— "All the chief expressions exhibited by man are the same throughout the world. The fact is interesting, as it affords a new argument in favour of *the several races being descended from a single parent stock.*"

Such was the opinion of a few among the greatest scientific names of the 19th century, with whom Professor Huxley

---

* See Appendix U.

was evidently unacquainted, as he boasted he did not know a single person who believed what is so plainly recorded in the Bible, that unerring Word, which has God for its author, truth without mixture of error for its matter, and the happiness of mankind for its end. Leaving, therefore, this veritable and learned Ishmaelite to his own devices, I pass on to notice briefly two more of Darwin's disciples who claim to be your cousins, as they both happen to be denizens of that great country, which has been so finely described by a distinguished American statesman as "bounded on the north by the Aurora Borealis, on the east by the rising sun, on the west by the horizon, and on the south as far as we choose to go!"

Professor Andrew Jackson Davis may be regarded as the Huxley of the Far West in respect of *Darwinism* and the *Origin of Man*, only he claims to have acquaintanceship with the spirit world, which the latter despises, and so, of course, can make no pretensions to stellar learning. The American professor is known to be the founder of the "Pantheon of Progress"—a magnificent temple on the banks of the Hudson river, which, in the comprehensive language of its architect, "covers an immense field of beautiful conceptions, also boundless regions of psychological problems and of scientific discoveries innumerable"—and author of several works relating to "Spiritualism" and the "Origin of Man." Hence, Professor Davis, in his *Principles of Nature*, teaches that "MATTER is the substance of every thing in the universe, and it is a law of Nature to produce its ultimate result, viz., the MIND."

In his description of the "Pantheon of Progress," Professor Davis tells his visitors that they will meet in his Halls of Science with *Brahma*, "the representative idealist"—*Sanconiatho*, "the divine friend of mankind," and many other ancient celebrities; notably *Moses*, "the reputed author of certain personal bye-

laws (viz., the Decalogue) and egotistic
institutions. But whether he lived or
not," the lively professor paradoxically
remarks, "is a question of no importance,
for he lives in the 'Pantheon of Progress,'
together with *Jesus Christ*, of whom too
little is really known for an honest man
to affirm any thing as positively true."

In his *Principles of Nature*, the learned
professor tells his readers that it is by
spiritualism that he has acquired his amaz-
ing stock of knowledge. "I pass," he says,
"from the body with a desire for a
particular kind of information. This
desire attracts the particular kind of
information from all other things, and
causes it to flow into the mind;" and
he adds, with natural pride, as lifting him
above ordinary professors like Huxley
or Haeckel—"I can converse with the
spirits distinctly, and learn from them
the peculiar impressions and affections
of their souls."

The professor, thus taught by the spirits,
proceeds to instruct his fellow-creatures

on the various subjects of MATTER, MIND, and MAN in the following lucid way.

"MATTER," taught the American professor, "is the substance of every thing in the universe, and it is a law of Matter to produce its ultimate, viz., MIND. As the first power of motion contained all forces known to exist, so did Matter contain the specific properties to produce MAN, who is the most perfect combination of organised matter. There are only two existing principles—one, *the body ;* the other, *the soul :* one, *the divine Positive mind ;* the other, *the Univercœlum.* MAN is a part of this great body of the Divine Mind. He is a gland, or minute organ, *the earth being to him as a stomach.* Sound conveys to the mind a peculiar vibration, which irresistibly undulates the portion of the mind with which it comes in contact, and this vibration is *the idea.*

" MAN was originally *an oyster,* or clam, from which he has progressed to his present condition ; this oyster produced a *tadpole* (possibly the same as Darwin's ascidian tadpole), which produced *a qua-druped*, which produced *a baboon*, which produced *an orang-outang*, which produced *a negro*, which produced a *white man*. Man as yet is only half developed; there being still six gradations through which he has to pass before he becomes a perfect mortal, and fit to share the bliss of the seventh sphere. The original inhabitants of the earth were black; the subsequent nations were *brown;* the branches of these were *red*, from these spread the *yellow;* and from these developed the *white man*."

The investigations of Professor Davis have not been confined to the inhabitants of the earth. By means of the spirits he has been enabled to make a survey of the Planetary Worlds; and to tell his disciples what he has seen in each. The inhabitants of the planets he considers belong to the *genus homo*, but are in no way connected with yourselves. *E.g.:* Those of *Saturn* are "morally and intellectually perfect; " those of *Jupiter*, "in size, symmetry and beauty of form, exceed those of the inhabitants of the earth, walking like quadrupeds, by a modest desire to be seen only in an inclined posture, which has thus become an established position amongst them." The people of *Mars* are in a "much more exalted state than the inhabitants of the earth, and their hair, instead of growing on their heads, envelopes their necks" like a lady's boa. Those who inhabit *Venus* are "a barbarous, savage and giant-like community, much given to cannibalism." Whilst those of *Mercury* "much more nearly resemble orang-outangs than human beings."

Such are the results of a personal exploration of the planets by a transcendental philosopher from the Far West. But I must not omit to remind you that there is an important distinction between the conclusions of the two learned *savans*, Darwin and Davis, respecting the primeval ancestor of MAN; for whereas the former is content to trace your pedigree only to the larvæ of an *ascidian tadpole*, the latter goes one step further back, and declares that the true origin of man is to be found in that delicious mollusc—*the native oyster !*

Professor Lesley, likewise from the land of the Far West, in his work entitled *Man's Origin and Destiny Sketched from the Platform of the Sciences*, without entering into the same minute details as his brother-professors, Darwin and Davis, have done, arrives at a similar conclusion, and so contents himself with affirming that he has discovered " sufficient evidence (though he is very reticent as to the *how, where,* and *when*) to prove that *man is a developed monkey*" (p. 93). But you may judge of his incapacity to form an opinion on such a subject, when you hear that he once committed himself to the glaring absurdity of declaring that "the faculty of worship in itself is no distinction between man and beast, because *the devotion of a dog to his master is the same as that of a Christian to his Saviour, or an angel to his God*" !

The ignorance displayed by Professor Lesley whenever there is any allusion to the sacred writings of the Jews, is such as to deprive his testimony of all value whatever on the subject of *Man's Origin Sketched from the Platform of the Sciences;* as you will judge from the following specimen of his hermeneutical powers.   On the subject of *Unity of Race,* this Yankee professor declares that " there is absolutely *no reason* for supposing the white and black and red races to be of one species, except *an absurd legend ascribed* to an ancient Semitic lawgiver (Moses). The legend of Adam and Eve makes all mankind descend from Cain first, and Seth afterwards; and that after the antediluvians were all destroyed, Noah and his family become in their turn the sole progenitors of all our present races.   *This hotch-potch of old Hebrew legends—this tissue of absurdity called the Biblical history of the origin of mankind,* is absolutely the sole and entire argument for not considering the human race as much distinct in kind

P

and origin, as are the American bison and the European cow." *

Such was the reasoning of a Yankee infidel, who called himself a scientific investigator of the "Origin of Man." Considering that the greatest minds of all time, of any age, and of all climes, such as Francis Bacon, John Milton and Isaac Newton, contradicted practically the silly utterances of this bumptious American, who has done his utmost to degrade the name of "Professor," you will not wonder if I apply the words of a very eminent Englishman, Robert Hall, as peculiarly applicable to this wretched scoffer of the infallible truths of the Bible:—"Ignorance the most profound, joined to dogmatism the most presumptuous, is the marked characteristic" of Professor Lesley's unhappy creed.

But he did not stand alone in his folly; as there existed in his time, in the chief city of the American Republic, a Society,

---

* See Appendix V.

of which Lesley may have been the most noted member, belonging to that class of boasting Infidels called " Posi-tivists," which was known as—

" *The First Positivist Society of New York,*" whose pseudo-religious principles were thus defined by themselves—" Scientific Religion; the Dynamic Theory of the Universe; Time and Space explained; FORCE and its changes to account for all Phenomena; and of a new System of Morals."

I will not, Gentlemen, insult your un-derstandings by thinking that you will deem this silly craze of the New York Infidels other than devoid of all approach to common sense and simple reason, but I refer to it for the purpose of exposing the depth of folly, to which some pretenders to the name of *savans* could descend in their wild speculations during the 19th century. And I will content myself with pointing out that these would-be regene-rators of humanity have compressed their creed into forty Articles; adding, however, to these "forty stripes" an important *Appendix*, which "taken together covers the whole of human activity, thought and emotion, and places life and progress and reform upon a solid basis." And they inaugurate their Positivist system by positively declaring that—"It is no longer possible for an honest enquirer to accept as true any of the prevalent religions. Therefore, *the great need of the age* is a thorough and entire change of human thoughts, feelings, hopes and interests, from theological subjective and illusory suppositions of Hebrew and Christian mythology, to the modern objective, practical and positive conclusions, previsions and rewards of science."

The doctrine so grandly announced by these New York Positivists appears to have been something similar to the protoplastic theories of Professor Huxley, only called by a different name—viz., that of *Cellular Genesis*, which is invented to explain another hypothesis dignified by the title of *Osmosis*, which is in its turn to explain *every thing*, whether of a celestial, terrestrial or subterranean nature. These smatterers, following in the wake of Louis Büchner, the German doctor of FORCE, whom an eminent *savant* once justly pronounced as belonging to "the weaker brethren," affirm that the real secret of life and growth is the play of Force called *Osmosis, i.e.,* "filtration."

Thus it appears that *Osmosis* is the new religion of the Positivists of New York, which is to decide every thing. They are more advanced in scepticism than that noted warrior, of whom it is related that on going into battle he was wont to pray, " O God, if there be a God, save my soul, if I have a soul ! " which elicited from the Jacobite Bishop Atterbury, on hearing this anecdote, another of a different nature—as it reminded him of a story told of a braver warrior, who was wont at the commencement of any engagement to offer a prayer to the following effect—" O God, if in the heat of battle I forget *Thee*, do not Thou forget *me !* " For these pseudo-scientists ignore Deity, and reject the possibility of the conditional "if" altogether. Man, whom they consider to be merely an aggregate of molecular cells, made up of carbon with a dash of phosphorus, and the human will to be only a succession of cellular vibrations, these altogether constitute the grand cosmological theory of Osmosis, and that in the estimation of these New York Positivists is every thing. Thus it comes to pass that immortality, the future life, all your hopes, passions, desires, fears and aspirations—all duty, sensation, reflection, memory and will—all that ever has been, is now, and ever will be—all things human and divine, may be summed up in the one sole idea of these unscientific sciolists, viz., the all potent doctrine of OSMOSIS! And there comes a shout and a roar from the region of the Far West, like that which once stirred the passions of the idolatrous Ephesians in the Temple of Diana—*Great is* OSMOSIS *of the New York Positivists ! ! !*

A portrait of these boasters of the 19th century has been so well drawn by one of your own poets, that I cannot forbear quoting some of the lines, in order to give you a just idea of these would-be philosophers, as entertained by every man endowed with common sense, and unaffected by the bold and glaring Atheism of that much-lauded age.

" Life and the Universe show spontaneity ;
Down with ridiculous notions of Deity !
Churches and creeds are all lost in the mists :
TRUTH must be sought with the *Positivists !*
If you are pious (mild form of insanity),
Bow down and worship the mass of humanity ;
Other religions are buried in mists,
We're our own gods, say the Positivists.
There was an APE in the days that were earlier ;
Centuries passed, and his hair became curlier :
Centuries more gave a thumb to his wrist—
Then he was Man, and a POSITIVIST." *

You have heard now how the American Positivists have elected FORCE to be their

---

* See Mr. Mortimer Collins' lines in his *British Birds, by the Ghost of Aristophanes.*

god, while they argue that this power having brought a fortuitous concourse of atoms together, men, together with everything else in the universe, have been gradually evolved from it. And it is evident that all these three theories virtually reject the simple and majestic statement of Scripture—"And God said, Let us make man in our image, after our likeness......So God created man in His own image, in the image of God created He him; male and female created He them" (Gen. i. 26, 27).

To speak of man having been· evolved from a tadpole, instead of being a separate act of creative power by an all-wise and Omnipotent Being, is not necessarily infidel, but it is certainly as opposed to God's written word, as it is to His works. Happy would it be if all Evolutionists could see the force of what Dr. M'Cosh has said in his *Method of the Divine Government*—"Science has a foundation, and so has religion. Let them unite their foundations, and the basis will be broader, and they will be two compartments of one great fabric reared to the glory of God."

To declare, however, that life has been evolved from dead matter, whether in the shape of a piece of carbon or a fortuitous concourse of atoms, can only be described, in the expressive words of the late Thomas Carlyle, as "deluded insanity." Hence the saying of Humboldt's just rebuke of Strauss, and which is equally applicable to multitudes of Evolutionists in the present day—"What displeases me in Strauss," said one of Germany's greatest philosophers, "is the scientific levity which causes him to see no difficulty in the organic springing from the inorganic—nay, man himself from the Chaldean mud." ! ! !

Professor Lionel Beale has forcibly exposed this "deluded insanity," by remarking that "the declaration again and again repeated, and now taught even to children, that the living and the non-living differ only in degree, that the living has been evolved by degrees from the non-living, and that the latter passes by gradations towards the former state—no one has adduced any evidence in proof of these conclusions, which are, in fact, dictatorial assertions only, and *no specimen of any kind of matter which is actually passing from the non-living to the living state*, or which can be shewn to establish any connection between these absolutely different conditions of matter, *has been or can be at this time brought forward.* We must not allow the mind to be diverted by fanciful comparisons and asserted resemblances of the living to the non-living, from the careful consideration of the real differences between that which is alive, and that which is not."*

Happily, Mr. Darwin's "hypothesis" is not affected by the above remarks; but I may venture to quote the following from a paper in *Blackwood* of Nov. 1874, entitled, *Modern Scientific Materialism*, as a fair and impartial judgment of the illustrious deceased.

---

* Lecture on *Dictatorial Scientific Utterances and the Decline of Thought*, before the Victoria Institute, by Professor Lionel Beale, F.R.S.

"Darwin is an accomplished Naturalist, with rare powers of observation, and an entertaining and often graceful power of describing the results of his prolonged investigations. But the importance of the principle has been greatly overrated. Darwin is as little of a philosopher as any man who ever lived. His genius is one of observation and narration, with very faint powers of argument, and with no depth of synthetic insight. He fails frequently to understand the true meaning of the facts which he describes, and still more frequently the higher conclusions to which they lead. He is weak in logic, and especially weak in every attempt to rise into the higher region, which he sometimes essays, of abstract discussion. If Darwin* and Herbert Spencer and others

---

* The French *savans* do not recognise Mr. Darwin's claims in the same way as Professor Huxley and others do at home. I believe he was rejected three times from admission into the French Academy, on account of the *unscientific* nature of his theories.

were really the great philosophers which
their admirers declare them to be, then their
intellectual character may be safely left to
the future.   They do not need to have .
their merits emblazoned as on a signpost,
for the applausive gaze of the common
herd " (p. 529).

I believe there is too much truth in the
phrase which Mr. Wendell Holmes has
applied to Darwin, and Huxley, and
Herbert Spencer and others, that they
constitute " THE MUTUAL ADMIRATION SO-
CIETY." They are so frequently in the
habit of praising each other, that it has
ceased to be of any value. And when
Huxley talks about Darwin being the
greatest philosopher since Aristotle, a title
which Professor Owen, with far better
judgment, as we have already pointed out,
ascribed to Cuvier, we are inclined to
smile, when we recollect that in the first
edition of Darwin's *Origin of Species* the
author sagely intimated that · *the whole*
might have been formed by *Natural Selection* out of a bear that was once seen

swimming about in deep water like a whale, with his mouth wide open catching flies! But that memorable passage expressive of the author's preference for speculation over science was withdrawn in the second edition, and has not, I believe, appeared since.*

The most crushing blow which the Evolution theory ever received was in the brilliant address of Dr. Virchow, Professor of Pathology in the University of Berlin, at the Munich Conference of German professors (September, 1877), when the opinion of the greatest living authority on the subject was thus delivered—"As a matter of fact," said the learned Virchow, "we must positively recognize that as yet there exists a sharp line of demarcation between man and the ape. We cannot teach—*we cannot pronounce it to be a conquest of science, that man descends from the ape or from any other animal whatever.*"

---

* See Appendix W.

Undeterred by this solemn warning on the part of a master, Mr. Kay-Robinson hastened into the midst of the fray—

"As fools rush in where angels fear to tread"—

by assuming that in consequence of Darwin having so successfully proved man *in the past* to have originally been evolved primarily from a tadpole, and finally from an old-world monkey amongst your prehistoric ancestors, it had been given him to declare and teach what *the Man of the Future* would become by the logical outcome of the Evolutionary theory. In imitation of a very clever skit by the late Lord Lytton on *the Coming Race*, in which he advocates "Woman's Rights," and supposes that hereafter woman would be the stronger and superior vessel, and, in short, that then woman would be every thing, and man next to nothing, Mr. Kay-Robinson once drew in *The Nineteenth Century* the not very flattering picture, or rather, as we might appropriately term it, the ludicrous caricature of the poor wretch, once a man, as he will be after the 20th century, according to the pseudo-scientists of that age.

"The Man of the Future," he said, "will be a toothless, hairless, slow-limbed animal, incapable of extended locomotion. His feet will have no divisions between the toes. He will be very averse to fighting, and will maintain his position in the foremost files of time to come solely upon the strength of one or two peculiar convolutions in his brain."

Mr. Kay-Robinson, undeterred by the wise warning of the cautious judge to a hasty friend, "Give your conclusions, but not your reasons," propounded his fanciful theory respecting *the Man of the Future*, on the ground that the Darwinian theory of Evolution must be true as regards the human race in the past, alleging, with the usual assurance of the sceptical school, that—

"No man of thought can honestly deny that his (Darwin's) genealogy of the human race is in the main reconcilable with *fact*, with *science*, and with *religion* ! ! !

.... Each individual, before coming into the world, exemplifies in his own person the development of his species from some lower animal, lower even than the ape, and furnishes solid collateral evidence of the truth of the theory founded upon a comparison of the affinities and differences of allied species as they exist at present"!!!*

It may be a doubtful point to decide whether the author of the above passage was writing seriously, humorously, or sarcastically, but if seriously it is a fresh instance of the self-illusion which has weakened the minds of so many speculators in the present day. To assert that *fact*, *science*, and *religion* all support the Darwinian theory, is an astonishing sign of the contempt for exact truth which certain writers display. As Johnson once said of Lord Monboddo's theory, "Of a standing *fact* there ought to be no controversy. If there are men with tails,

---

* *The Nineteenth Century* for May, 1883.

why don't they show them?" But, in truth, all *facts* are against Mr. Darwin's hypothesis that man is a developed monkey.

We are warranted in asserting with the most unswerving confidence, that all observation, experience, testimony, and I hope I may add without giving offence, common sense likewise, like *religion* itself, contradict Mr. Robinson's assertion of *facts* affording any support to the Evolutionary theory. And as for *science*, let the brief sayings of a jury of the most distinguished scientists, half natives and half foreigners, decide how far he is entitled to claim science on behalf of his untenable theory.

ENGLISH SCIENTISTS.

1. *Sir David Brewster.*—" The theory concerning *Protoplasm* is a dangerous and degrading speculation."

2. *Sir Richard Owen.*—" No instance of *change* of one species into another has ever been recorded by man."

3. *St. George Mivart.*—" The Darwinian

hypothesis is beset with certain scientific difficulties, which are absolutely *insuperable.*"

4. *Dr. Elam.*—"Organic Evolution is a mere *figment* of the intellect."

5. *Thomas Carlyle.*—"The Evolution theory is deluded *insanity.*"

6. *Frank Buckland.*—"The doctrines of *so-called* Evolution and Development have seemingly gained ground of late, but I have too much faith in the good sense of my fellow-countrymen to think that these tenets will be very *long lived.*"

FOREIGN SCIENTISTS.

1. *Agassiz.*—"Man does *not* descend from the mammals which preceded him in the Tertiary age."

2. *Humboldt.*—"The scientific levity with which some talk of man being evolved from the Chaldean mud is *most degrading.*"

3. *De Quatrefages.*—"Man *cannot* be the descendant of any Simian type whatever."

4. *Carruthers.*—"*No* single case of Evo-

lution of one species into another has ever come within the observation of man."

5. *Virchow.*—" Man has *not* descended from the ape, or from any other animal whatever."

6. *Barraude.*—" The theoretical Evolution of the trilobite is *a mere figment* of the imagination, without any foundation *in fact.*"

It will be observed, that the conclusion which these distinguished *savans* have unanimously come to, adverse to the Darwinian theory, rests upon the fact that there is not one single instance in the files of geological time, embracing it may be millions of years, of one species, extinct or extant, in the act of turning into another. Hence the *Times* once remarked somewhat severely on this patent failure of the hypothesis—

" This is precisely the solution which Mr. Darwin is unable to apply to his instances of his approximation between species. If he could say in a single instance, *solvitur ambulando,* here is a case

Q 2

of one true species having passed into another, we should have a practical proof that the kind of approximation he brings to light is of such a kind as to end in coincidence. But this is what he has not done. It is not a little curious that the finite time which Newton demands is the very condition most energetically repudiated by Mr. Darwin and his followers. They place no limit whatever to the amount of time which their process requires. We are reminded by such speculations, of the famous story which Corporal Trim endeavoured so effectually to recite to Uncle Toby. 'There was a certain king of Bohemia,' said Trim, 'but in whose reign, except his own, I am not able to inform your honour.'—'There was a certain monkey,' says Mr. Darwin; of that he is quite sure, and he frequently reiterates the assurance; 'but in what period or country except his own, I am not able to inform my readers.' The certainty, unfortunately, is hypothetical, and the particular monkey unknown."

Having thus seen the opinions of so many eminent scientists adverse to the Evolution theory, let me quote the opposite opinion in the words of those who appear to be its ardent supporters. Nevertheless, the most illustrious of them all seems to have serious doubts regarding the soundness of his own special theory.

1. *Darwin.*—" To suppose that the eye could have been formed by Natural Selection, seems *absurd* in the highest possible degree."

2. *Tyndall.*—" It is certain that the Darwinian theory of Evolution must undergo modifications."

3. *Huxley.*—" It is more profitable to go wrong with Haeckel, than to stand still."

4. *Haeckel.*—" Worms originated by means of spontaneous generation from the inorganic compounds of carbon, &c., and are the direct ancestors of man."

5. *Louis Büchner.* — " The Evolution theory is perfectly irreconcilable with the idea of a *personal* Almighty Creator."

6. *Seeley.*—" The whole science of *Evolution* had grown out of the abandonment of this notion of *design.*"

7. *Carl Vögt* is reported to have told Darwin with logical justice, that his " theory turns the Creator out of doors, and leaves no room for the agency of such a Being; for the first living germ being granted, the process of Evolution necessarily follows. Man is not a special creation, produced in a different way, and distinct from other animals; but, on the contrary, *man* is only the highest product of the progressive evolution of animal life *springing from the group of apes next below him.*"

Notwithstanding the apparent difference in the teaching of these two parties, the twelve Anti-Darwinites, and the seven pro-Darwinites, Professor Huxley tells the clergy assembled at Sion College to hear his address in 1867, " The views, of which I as the Minister of Science am the exponent to night, are held by men who are as Christian in motive and practice as you. These doctrines are held by the best of men; they are held out of no wantonness, or irreverence, or eccentricity. They are held by men who seek to discover to themselves and to present to others Scientific Truth. I ask you to remember this, to consider this; and *then I ask you to judge us.*" *

Bearing in mind the important distinction between the teaching of Darwin, who believes in a Supreme Creator, who first gave life to those who had it not; and the teaching of men like Haeckel, or Büchner, or Carl Vögt, who distinctly deny the existence of such a Being, we regret to be compelled to observe, that those of the clergy who have studied both sides of the question differ as much from Huxley respecting what is " Scientific Truth," as they do on the rightful interpretation of the doctrines of the Bible. He is evidently unable to see what is so evident to unprejudiced

---

* *Transactions of Victoria Inst.*, vol. ii., p. 329.

observers, who regard Scripture as a Revelation from God to man; containing nothing but infallible truth; and that it is quite impossible for the works of God to contradict each other. What is often called "Scientific Truth" in respect to Geology has often proved erroneous, as we have already seen; and then it has to be retracted, set aside and forgotten. At best it is a mere series of conjectures, which time has often refuted before, and will doubtless refute again. Geology differs essentially from mathematical science. We can only reason with certainty from cause to effect; and when men attempt to draw inferences from effect to cause, as in Geology or Creation, men can only conjecture. Hence, when Professor Huxley truly says that "the Methods of all Sciences are—1. *Observation of facts;* 2. Comparison and classification; 3. Deduction; 4. *Verification;*" * you have seen how completely the

---

* Huxley's *Lay Sermons*, p. 92.

Evolution theory breaks down under such tests. In regard to the first and last of these rules, that *the observation of facts* is dead against the Evolution theory; for notwithstanding the frequent challenges, the promoters have never been able to observe one single instance, in all the millions of years invented in support of the theory, of one species of animal life turning into another. And as for *verification*, the syllogistic reasoning of Dr. Elam, before quoted, is indeed unanswerable: "Without verification, a theoretic conception is a mere figment of the intellect. The theory of organic Evolution is an unverified theoretic conception. Therefore, organic Evolution is a mere figment of the intellect."

I have now, Gentlemen, endeavoured to set before you the opinions of a considerable number of the *savans* of the 19th century, respecting the doctrines of Mr. Charles Darwin on the subjects of EVOLUTION and DEVELOPMENT; and I venture to think you will scarcely wonder at the fact that the really wise, belonging to the two centuries which have intervened between that age and the present day, have utterly and entirely rejected that singular delusion, which made man the lineal descendant of the larvæ of an ascidian tadpole; though it never should be forgotten that on the subject of the Evolution theory the gulf is far wider, and the difference is far greater, between Darwin's hypothesis and that of his infidel followers, than it is between his teaching and the creed of those who accept the Mosaic Cosmogony as revealed in the inspired Word of God; and that, with the exception of Professor Tyndall, every one of them is more or less hostile to the speculations of the great Naturalist, who towards the close of his life candidly acknowledged that the Evolution theory was " only an hypothesis."

In the peroration to his brilliant Essay on the *Use and Limit of the Imagination in Science*, Professor Tyndall says—

" When we endeavour to pass from the

phenomena of physics to those of thought, we meet a problem which transcends any conceivable expansion of the powers which we now possess. We stand at length face to face with the Incomprehensible. The territory of physics is wide, but it has its limits, from which we look with vacant gaze into the region beyond. *Whence come we? whither go we? The question dies without an answer—without even an echo— upon the infinite shores of the Unknown*" (p. 72).

I believe the distinguished and fair-dealing author of the above words to be mistaken in declaring that the important questions, "Whence come we?" and "Whither go we?" die without an answer or an echo. At least, some great men of different ages have thought otherwise. If the author of Hamlet once declared, "We know what we are; but know not what we may be," John Sterling, as related by his biographer, Thomas Carlyle, makes this reply—"I affirm we do know whence we come, and whither we go;" as John Wesley taught amid the twilight of the 18th century—" I am," he said, " the creature of to-day, passing through life as an arrow through the air. I am a spirit come from God, and returning to God; just hovering over the great gulf, till a few moments hence I am no more seen. I drop into an unchangeable eternity. I want to know *one thing*, the way to heaven, and how to land safe on that happy shore."

One word, in conclusion, Gentlemen, in reference to the EVOLUTION THEORY, which has so long engaged our attention. I cannot help thinking that if ever the scientific speculations, and I must add " delusions" as well, are ever impartially and fully written, it will prove the truth of Bacon's axiom, that " *In all superstitions wise men follow fools.*" There is as much superstition and more credulousness on the part of those who prefer their own crude imaginations to the teaching of revealed religion, than in that of the most confiding

Papist who believes in the "Infallibility"
of the Pope, or the most benighted Negro,
who practically makes feticism his god.
There is sufficient evidence that the "fools
of the 18th century, as the Psalmist of old
terms them, who virtually said, "There is
no God," led the professedly wise of the
19th century into all the follies, paradoxes,
and extravagant speculations of those who
ignored Scripture, despised history, which
Bolingbroke once justly defined as "Philosophy teaching by example;" and who
were content to accept the dogma of a
famous lay preacher of that day, which
may be regarded as the Shibboleth of the
party's creed, viz., "Scepticism is the
highest of duties; blind faith the one
unpardonable sin."*

Permit me, then, to reply to this strange
paradox, to quote what a more famous
preacher than Professor Huxley has said
on this subject, as his words are weighty,
and deserving of your most serious atten-

* Huxley's *Lay Sermons*, p. 21.

tion: "The wrath of God," wrote the
Apostle Paul, more than 20 centuries ago,
"is revealed from heaven against all who
hold the truth in unrighteousness. Because
that which may be known of God is manifest in them; for God hath showed it unto
them.   For the invisible things of Him
from the creation of the world are clearly
seen, being understood by the things that
are made, even His eternal power and
Godhead; *so that they are without excuse.*
Because that, when they knew God, they
glorified Him not as God, neither were
thankful; but became vain in their imaginations, and their foolish heart was dark-
ened.   Professing themselves to be wise,
they became fools, and changed the truth
of God into a lie, and worshipped and
served the creature more than the Creator,
who is blessed for ever.   AMEN."

And so, Gentlemen, if I may no longer
in the interests of Science and Truth call
you by the endearing name of relations or
kinsfolk, I trust we may part as "friends;"
and as such I have the honour to bid you,

with feelings of deep regret at our parting, in the language of one of your own poets—

> " Farewell!
> A long farewell to all my greatness ! "

No sooner were these last words uttered than the NEANDERTHAL SKULL vanished from my view: a low groan of indescribable anguish ran through the assembly, which gradually grew into a mighty roar. It seemed as if Bedlam were let loose, and that I was transported to some unknown region, resembling one of the most stormy scenes in the French Republican Assembly, such as it was thus graphically described by the Parisian Journals of July 8th, 1873 : "At these words the whole left arose. M. le Serve stormed; M. Locroy shook both his fists; the uncouth Col. Langlois was furious; the mild M. Schœlcher precipitated himself to the foot of the tribune. M. de Lafayette was in a state bordering on delirium; deputies stamped, kicked, shouted, &c.; and this tempest lasted for at least ten minutes, and then the angry discussion continued."

The clatter and chatter and din were waxing fast and furious in the assembly of Evolutionists and their opponents, gathered on that bright summer evening of 2085, in St. James' Hall, Piccadilly; when as the uproar became louder and louder, I suddenly awoke, and found it was all a DREAM!

P.S.—Since writing the above treatise, the chief portion of which was done about 14 years ago, I have had an opportunity, through the kindness of the Rev. Horace Noel, of reading his recent and most instructive pamphlet, entitled, *The Testimony of a Dewdrop to its Creator*. Within the compass of a little more than one-third of the pamphlet, which constists of only 63 pages, he gives an admirable compendium of the arguments whereby the Evolutionists attempt to ignore or deny the existence of a Supreme Creator, as well as proving how completely they have failed in their lawless attempts. The only mistake which the author has made is attributing to Darwin, as Strauss does, what more properly belongs to many of his disciples, like Professors Huxley and Haeckel. For not only did the late Mr. Darwin cordially acknowledge the existence of a Supreme Creator, but he bore testimony to the value of Christian missions in raising man from that degraded state to which man must assuredly fall, as long as he is without the knowledge of the true God.

The admission of the infidel Strauss, who for a time—happily for a short time only—misled that admirable and peerless royal lady, the much-beloved and much-lamented Princess Alice, is quoted by Mr. Noel with great effect. Strauss once wrote with perfect truth as follows:—

"We see that in organic nature like always proceeds from like, never unlike from unlike. . . . . . Natural science observed the different species of organic beings as inviolable limits, admitting perforce the development of varieties and

R

domestic breeds, but declaring the Evolution of one species into a really new and
different one *simply impossible.* If this is
so, then we must unquestionably take
refuge in the conception of creation and
of miracles; then God must have in the
beginning created grass and herbs and
trees, as well as animals, each after its
kind.

" Natural science has long endeavoured
to establish the Evolution theory in the
place of the conception of creation, so
alien to her spirit; but it was Charles
Darwin who made the first truly scientific
attempt to deal seriously with this conception, and trace it through the organic
world. . . . . Vainly did we philosophers
decree the extermination of miracles; our
ineffectual sentence died away, because we
could neither dispense with miraculous
agency, nor point to any natural force able
to replace it, where it had hitherto seemed
most indispensable. Darwin has demonstrated this force, this power of Nature;
he has opened the door by which *a happier*

*coming race will cast out miracles, never to
return. Every one who knows what miracles
imply will praise him in consequence, as one of
the greatest benefactors of the human race.*"
(p. 41) ! ! !

Mr. Noel remarks that "the above
passage is commendable, at any rate, for
its clearness and candour;" he might with
equal justice have added, a more stupen-
dous piece of folly, impiety, and untruth-
fulness was never penned by the most
daring and blaspheming Atheist since the
world began. The man who in the present
day can deny the fact of the miracles
recorded in Scripture, and patent to the
whole world, is nothing more or less than
an ignorant and intolerant bigot, who is
unworthy of the least notice. If any
Christian might think it worth while to
notice the delusion which has beclouded
the minds of infidels like Strauss and his
godless followers, we need only (1) point
to the Saviour's Resurrection from the
grave, on which the Christian religion
rests, and the certainty that in God's own

R 2

appointed time that religion will "cover the earth as the waters cover the seas." (2) The fact that the Japhetic race (which in general terms may be said to include Christendom) has for so long a period dominated the rest of the world, just as the prophecy of Noah foretold would be the case. (3) The existence and position of the race of Israel throughout the world at the present time, exactly as prophecy foretold, compared with the other great nations which were ruling 3000 years ago in the time of David and Solomon, and which have now perished from off the face of the earth. Where is Tyre?—as great a maritime power then as England is now. Where is the great Empire of the Hittites? —the records of whose power have only recently been brought to light. Where are the mighty kingdoms of Assyria, Babylonia, and Egypt? Echo mournfully answers, *Where?* The man who attempts to deny or to decry the miracles recorded in Scripture is deserving of the sharp reproof which Professor Tholuck of Germany once gave to the infidel Materialists of his day: "If a man is *a Materialist*, we Germans think he is *not educated.*" And we should not forget the advice of the wise King of Israel: "Answer a fool according to his folly, lest he be wise in his own conceit."

As Professor Tyndall truly said, in the peroration of his lecture at the Royal Institution in 1877, after describing a large number of experiments made by himself with the view of testing the theory of "spontaneous generation," "*From the beginning to the end of the enquiry there is not, as you have seen, a shadow of evidence in favour of the doctrine of spontaneous generation. There is, on the contrary, overwhelming evidence against it.*"

With equal truth the same may be said, *mutato nomine*, respecting the doctrine of man having been gradually evolved from lifeless matter like a bit of carbon.

Mr. Noel remarking on those weak-kneed Christians, who think it best to endeavour to compromise matters by admitting that

God *may* have made the world by the process of Evolution, asks them to consider "how gratuitous, as well as mischievous, it is to bring about a forced partnership between the Christian's faith in the Scripture and this bankrupt theory;" adding, with much force—

"It is but natural that those who do not believe in God should make the best they can of Evolution. But it does seem exceedingly useless for those who believe in a God, able to create by the direct word of His power, to think that He should have chosen to make a world by the cumbrous and clumsy process of Evolution. Wooden legs are made for people who are so unfortunate as to have lost their natural ones; and a man in this predicament may well be glad to wear the best wooden leg that can be made for him. But a man who has two good legs of his own, would scarcely have one of them cut off for the pleasure of wearing a wooden one, however artistically and highly recommended. Neither if believers in the God of the

Bible are wise, will they adopt the wooden leg of Evolution, by whatever parties it may be recommended. . . . . *The positive evidence of Scripture is against Evolution; whilst on the other side we have purely and simply a theory, whose whole strength depends on the foregone conclusion that miracles must, if possible, be ' exterminated'* " (p. 61).

APPENDICES.

APPENDICES.

APPENDIX A, PAGE 19.

Plutarch records of Sylla, who preceded Ovid by about half a century, that on his return from the Mithridatic war, as he was passing the Oracle called " Nymphœum," near Apollonia, there was brought before him a Satyr, which had been taken asleep, " exactly such as statuaries and painters represent to us." When Sylla questioned him in many languages who and what he was, " he could utter nothing intelligible ; his accent being harsh and inarticulate, something between the neighing of a horse and the bleating of a goat. Sylla was shocked at his appearance, and ordered him to quit his presence." From which we may conclude that " Satyrs," the creation of the ancient poets, were something like the missing link between man and beast, according to the Darwinian theory !

APPENDIX B, PAGE 29.

Max Müller's *Science of Language*, 177, 8 ; 5th edition. In the 8th edition of the same work, Max Müller wisely observed that " Lord Monboddo admits that *as yet* no animal has been discovered in the possession of language. . . . . . If, therefore, the science of language establishes a frontier between man and the brute *which can never be removed*, it would seem to possess peculiar claims on the attention of all who consider it their duty to enter their manly protest against a revival of *the shallow theories of Lord Monboddo*" (vol. i., p. 15).

APPENDIX C, PAGE 31.

Lamarck, *Phil. Zoolog.*, vol. ii., pp. 443, &c. The Rev. John Duns, F.R.S.E., in his *Biblical Natural Science*, has remarked on Lamarck's theory of a small gelatinous body being transformed into an oak or an ape and an orang-outang, after having been evolved out of a monad, slowly developing itself into the attributes and dignity of man, that "it would be hard to say whether the folly or the blasphemy in this system is greater" (vol. i., p. 545).

APPENDIX D, PAGE 46.

As a specimen of the scientific jargon current in the present day, I quote the words of Professor KÖLLIKERS on the subject of *Agamogenesis*, or "Alternate Generation," of which he writes as follows, commencing with the usual Darwinian IF :—

"IF a *Bipannaria*, a *Brachialaria*, a *Plutéus*, is competent to produce the *Echinoderm*, which is so widely different from it; IF a hydroid polype can produce the higher *Medusa;* IF the *Vermiform* Trematode 'nurse' can develop within itself the very unlike *Cercaria, it will not appear impossible* that the egg, or ciliated embryo, of a spunge for once, under special conditions, might become a *hydroid polype,* or the embryo of a *Medusa,* an *Echinoderm." !!!* Professor Huxley, in his *Lay Sermons,* p. 341, opposes this view.

APPENDIX E, PAGE 53.

Origin of Species, p. 186. The late Lord Chancellor Hatherly, in a letter to the author of *All the Articles of the Darwinian Faith,* says—

"I believe your mode of treating the preposterous fictions of Darwin is the only way to shake the self-confident tone of would-be philosophers. Newton's grandest saying, after 'Deus non est Æternitas sed Æternus,' was 'Hypotheses non fingo.' Newton kept back his *Principia* for years, because a mistake had been made in an arc of the meridian, so closely did he keep to experimental truth. Now the crude fancy, nothing like so ingenious as the Ptolemaic cycles, because the Darwin fancy stumbles at every step, is exalted to a rank exceeding that of the discovery of gravitation. In a clever sermon by Pritchard, Savilian Professor at Oxford, preached before the British Association, he exposes the folly of this stuff, and proves that the chances against the eye being formed by development are more in number than Darwin's work being taken by the printer to pieces and tumbled into a bag, and then thrown back on the table in the same order that they came."

APPENDIX F, PAGE 58.

Descent of Man, i. 207 ; ii. 389. At p. 321, a tribe of the Japanese called "*the Ainos*," are mentioned as the most hairy race in the world. *Both Sexes*, according to Mr. Satow of the British Legation at Yedo some years ago, appear to have *beards ;* those of the males present a magnificent bushy appearance, sometimes attaining the length of 14 inches.

APPENDIX G, PAGE 78.

I have to-day (Jan. 26) received a communication from the President of the College of Surgeons in Dublin, in which he kindly replies to a question asked respecting Dr. Wolff's broad statement quoted in the text—showing that it is not correct; and concluding with the simple expression, "no real tail extant."

APPENDIX H, PAGE 89.

Professor Huxley faithfully copies the master in his indulgent use of the little "if." Thus he writes— "IF man be separated by no greater structural barrier from the brutes than they are from one another, *then it seems to follow* that IF any process of physical causation can be discovered by which the genera and families of ordinary animals have been produced, that process of causation is amply sufficient to account for the origin of man. IF it could be shown that the Marmosets are modified ramifications of a primitive stock, *then* there would be no rational ground for doubting that man *might have originated* by the gradual modification of a man-like ape. . . . I adopt Mr. Darwin's hypothesis, therefore, subject to the production of proof that physiological species *may be* produced by selective breeding." (*Evidence as to Man's Place in Nature*, pp. 105—8.) But this is the very thing which neither Darwin nor any of his disciples have ever been able to produce. His "hypothesis," then, necessarily falls to the ground.

APPENDIX I, PAGE 105.

So Mr. Charles Bray, in his *Manual of Anthropology*, p. 129, claims the merit of having introduced the theory of *Natural Selection* as far back as 1840, some years before Darwin's *Origin of Species* appeared. And Dr. M. Fuke, of Dublin, in his work on *Organism*, which was published at the same time, affirmed that "all living creatures were evolved from some primary creation of a few forms, or of one, into which life was first breathed by the Creator."

APPENDIX J, PAGE 112.

On the Genesis of Species, by St. George Mivart, F.R.S., pp. 5, 24. At p. 189 he calls attention to a grave mistake of Mr. Darwin, when he speaks in his *Origin of Species* of the "woodpecker (*Coloptes campestris*) having an organization quite at variance with its habits, and as never climbing a tree, though possessed of the special arboreal structure of other woodpeckers." It now appears, however, from the observations of Mr. W. H. Hudson, C.M.Z.S., that " its habits are in harmony with its structure."

Appendix K, page 136.

In the Second Series of his *Lectures on Language*, Max Müller observes of the "bow-wow" hypothesis, "the onomatopœic theory goes very smoothly as long as it deals with cackling hens and quacking ducks; but round that poultry yard there is a dead wall, and we soon find that it is behind that wall that language really begins."

Appendix L, page 138.

Chips iv., p. 470. Mr. Darwin here appears to agree with Professor Max Müller, as in his work on the *Descent of Man*, he says, "The Fuegians rank amongst the lowest barbarians; but I was continually struck with surprise how closely the three natives on board H.M.S. 'Beagle', who had lived some years in England, and could talk a little English, resembled us in disposition, and in most of our mental faculties. . . . . I was incessantly struck whilst living with the Fuegians on board the 'Beagle,' with the many little traits of character, showing how similar their minds were to ours; and so it was with a full-blooded negro with whom I happened once to be intimate " (vol. i., pp. 34, 232). Could Mr. Darwin say the same of the most intelligent dog, the wisest elephant, the most talkative parrot, or the most imitative monkey that ever lived, as he has said of the lowest savage? Surely this is conclusive against his theory, which he has truly termed " only an hypothesis."

APPENDIX M, PAGE 145.

Professor Tyndall should have added, "or the author of *Hamlet, Othello,* &c. In a newly-translated work (Dr. Benno Tschischwitz' *Shakespeare-Forschungen I.*, Halle, 1868), commenting on the philosophy of Giordano Bruno, the author notes Bruno's influence on the Elizabethan dramatists, and declares that Hamlet, when he compares " the sun breeding maggots in a dead dog to a god kissing carrion " (act ii., sc. 2, l. 181), is quoting Bruno's *Spaccio*. In Professor Tyndall's masterly Address at Belfast, as President of the British Association in 1874, there is an account of Bruno's Philosophy and the Atomic Doctrines, which introduced into England by Bruno, were followed, " in whole or in part, by Bacon, Descartes, Newton, &c., and their successors " (p. 26). Now it is remarkable that Bruno visited the court of Elizabeth from 1583—1586. Bacon had been called to the bar in 1581-2, after his wonderful University career; was fast rising in his profession when Bruno was in England, and his knowledge of Italian enabled him to read Bruno's works in Italian, and which have only been translated into English in the 19th century. Shakespeare came as a rustic lad, with a " little smattering of Latin and no Greek," in the year 1587, after Bruno had left England, to begin

S

earning his livelihood by holding gentlemen's
horses during their visit to the theatre. *Hamlet* was
entered, I believe, in what is now called "Sta-
tioners' Hall " A.D. 1602. Who was most likely to
have written it? Bruno was one who opposed the
Aristotlelian, which was then all powerful, both in
the Church and the world. He accepted the great
discovery of Copernicus; and held that memorable
contest at Oxford against the Aristotlelians, of which
G. H. Lewis has given such a graphic account in his
History of Philosophy from Thales to Comte. So rigid
was Oxford in favour of Aristotle, that her statutes
declared that Bachelors and Masters of Arts, who did
not faithfully follow Aristotle, were liable to a fine of
5*s.* for every point of divergence. Now it is an
interesting fact, that when at Cambridge, and only
fourteen years of age, Bacon had written vigorously
against the Aristotlelian philosophy, nearly ten years
before Bruno arrived in England.

APPENDIX N, PAGE 182.

Professor Huxley might have found another
lay philosopher 1000 years earlier than the time of
Bacon, on whom he might profitably have exercised
his wit, on account of his peculiar ideas respecting
Cosmogony. Cosmas, surnamed "Indicopleustes,"
a celebrated merchant of Alexandria in the sixth century, who subsequently became a monk, though not
a priest, after his travels had come to an end,
devoted himself during the remainder of his life to
proving what he considered the harmony between

Scripture and Science, by a great work, which was
not only to refute the "old wives' fable" of the
Antipodes, but was to form a complete system of
the universe, based upon the infallible teaching of
the Word of God. This wonderful book, entitled
*Topographia Christiana, or Christian Opinion concern-
ing the World,* opens with a tone of great confidence;
declaring itself to be "A Christian Topography of
the Universe," established by demonstrations from
Divine Scripture, concerning which "it is not lawful
for a Christian to doubt." In a similar strain
Cosmas proceeds to censure severely those weak-
kneed Christians who had allowed the subtleties of
Greek fables, or the deceitful glitter of mere human
science, to lead them astray; forgetting that Scripture contained intimations of the nature of the
universe of far higher value and authority than any
to which unassisted man could attain. His idea of
Cosmogony was as follows. The world was a flat
parallelogram; its length from east to west being
double its breadth from north to south. In the
centre is the earth we inhabit, surrounded by the
ocean, which is again encircled by another earth, in
which men lived before the Flood. To the north of
the world was a high conical mountain, around
which the sun and moon continually revolve.
When the sun is hid behind the mountain, it is
night; when it is on our side of the mountain, it is
day. To the edges of the outer earth the sky is
glued, consisting of four very high walls, rising to a
vast concave roof, and forming an immense edifice, of
which our world is the floor. This edifice is divided
into two stories by the firmament, which is placed

between the earth and the roof of the sky. The space above the firmament is occupied by the blest; and that below by the angels in their character of ministering spirits.

A few examples of the way by which Cosmas arrived at these astonishing conclusions may not be amiss. In Genesis v. 1, it is written, "This is the book of the generations of Adam;" expressions evidently intended to comprise every thing contained in the heaven and the earth. But as Cosmas contended, if the doctrine of the *Antipodes* were Scriptural and true, the sky would surround and contain the earth; and therefore Moses would only have said "This is the book of the generation of the sky." As many of the sacred writers had employed the term "the heavens and the earth" to denote the whole creation, Cosmas introduces them all—Abraham, David, Isaiah, &c., &c., even including Melchisedec, as having delivered their testimony against the existence of *the Antipodes*. Moreover, as the earth was said in Scripture to be firmly fixed in its foundations, Cosmas inferred that it could not by any possibility be suspended in the air, forgetful of the declaration, "God stretcheth out the north over the empty place, and *hangeth the earth upon nothing*" (Job xxvi. 7); and quite innocent of the fact that certain heathen writers several centuries previous had discovered this scientific truth. *E.g.*, Ovid says, "The earth, like a ball resting upon no support, hangs like a heavy weight upon the air beneath" (*Fasti*, vi. 8). And Lucan, a Spanish poet, murdered by Nero, pointedly speaks of "The earth being poised in empty air" (*Pharsalia*, v. 94). But Cosmas, undeterred by such heathen testimony, affirmed that as St. Paul stated that "God hath made of one blood all nations of men to dwell on all *the face* of the earth" (Acts xviii. 26), it clearly followed that men do not live on more faces than one, or upon the back! Hence, argues Cosmas, "with such a passage before his eyes, no Christian should ever dare to think or speak of *the Antipodes.*"

This curious work of Cosmas was published in the second volume of the Benedictine Edition of the Greek Fathers, Paris, 1706. And, strange to say, the arguments of Cosmas seen to have been adopted by a very wild writer of the 19th century, who bears one of the most illustrious names in English history, and who has got into many troubles by the violence of his language against those who believe in the Copernican system in general, and Newton's theory of gravitation in particular. He once wrote to ask me if I had any belief in that old scoundrel and rogue Sir Isaac Newton?!!!—the latter being, as is well known, one of the greatest and meekest among the sons of men.

I fear I have unintentionally done Professor Huxley some wrong, as since writing what I have said about his Address to the Clergy of Sion College, I have met with .a work entitled, *Remarks on Mosaic Cosmogony*, by B. W. Newton, in which the learned author (who was formerly an Oxford Fellow, and is now a minister of Christ, I believe, though not a clergyman of the Church of England) has proposed a new "Article of Faith" for general believers, part of which reads as follows:—"We believe and confess that God did, *in six literal days,* make the heavens and the earth, and all that in them is" (p. 102). The difficulty, of course, to the believer who has no knowledge of Hebrew consists in this, that in one place it is said that God made the heavens and the earth in one day (Genesis ii. 4); and in another that God made them "in six days" (Exodus xx. 11). To those who can distinguish between the Hebrew words translated "created" and "made," there is no difficulty.

APPENDIX O, PAGE 183.

See the *Spiritualist* of November 15th, 1871. The author once held the office for a short time, not of a regularly licensed curate, but of a casual in a cathedral town, where "Spiritualism" was once much in vogue; and though he was quite innocent of "chattering" with his follow-curates or old women of the place on the above-mentioned subject, he hopes the day will come when Professor Huxley will regret having thus needlessly insulted a class of persons, both male and female, who are very lightly esteemed both by themselves and the rest of the world.

APPENDIX P, PAGE 183.

The terms of "mild railing" and "ignorant invective," &c., of which Professor Huxley accuses his opponents, are mild compared with the "hard speeches" which his friends employ against those who decline to accept the Evolution theory. Dr.

Louis Büchner, in his *Force and Matter*, terms such persons—"mental slaves," "speculative idiots," and "yelping curs," while boasting of his own "enlightenment, and the forthcoming deliverances of his fellow-men from obsolete and pernicious prejudices" (p. 86).

Professor Haeckel, in his *Natural History of Creation*, declares that "Mankind are divided into two classes, those who believe in Evolution doctrines, and those who do not; the former being the thoughtful, and the latter the thoughtless" (p. 577). Would it not be better if Professor Huxley could follow the bright example of Professor Tyndall, who in his masterly articles on the so-called question of "spontaneous generation," has exhibited a courtesy towards opponents, which both Professor Huxley and many of the clergy in their heated controversial discussions would do well to imitate. See Tyndall's *Fragments of Science*, p. 562.

APPENDIX Q, PAGE 187.

If common sense did not assure us that the many passages in Scripture which treat on the subject, were to be understood in a metaphorical sense, those Evolutionists, who accept, as Mr. Darwin did, a Supreme Creator, who made the universe, and originally breathed life into one single form, might quote certain passages in the Book of Psalms and in Job in favour of the "beastly" or "worm" origin of man. Thus in the latter, which is probably the oldest book in the world, as old as

the Prisse Papyrus in the Louvre, and about five
centuries older than the Books of Moses, we read of
the saintly patriarch declaring, "I have said to
corruption, Thou art my father: to the *worm*, Thou
art my mother, and my sister" (Job xvii. 14).   And
so Bildad the Shuhite confirms the theory by asking
"How can man be clean that is born of a woman?
Behold even the stars are not pure in His sight.
How much less man, that is *a worm?* and the son of
man, which is *a worm*" (Job xxv. 4—6).   And so
the Psalmist, upwards of a thousand years later,
says, "I am *a worm*, and no man" (Ps. xxii. 6).
And in another place he thus candidly speaks of
himself, "So foolish was I, and ignorant: I was
as a beast before Thee" (Ps. lxxiii. 22).

APPENDIX R, PAGE 189.

There are three lines of descent in man's
pedigree, which may be respectively termed *Theistic,
Atheistic,* nad *Agnostic,* variously interpreted by Mr.
Charles Darwin, Professor Haeckel, and certain
American Agnostics as follows:—

The Theistic.	The Atheistic.	The Agnostic.
1. Larvæ of existing Ascidians.	A piece of Carbon.	Protoplastic atoms.
2. The Lancelet Fishes.	Animal Monera.	Ascidians.
3. Ganoids.	Worms.	Amphibians.
4. Lepidosiren.	Annelidæ.	Pentadactyle.
5. Amphibians.	Chordonia.	Hylobate.
6. Menotremata.	Ascidians.	Lemur.
7. Marsupials.	Kangaroos.	Platyrhine Monkey.

The Theistic.	The Atheistic.	The Agnostic.
8. Placentals.	Half Apes.	Anthropoid Apes.
9. Lemuridæ.	Tailed Apes.	Longimanous Apes.
10. Simiadæ.	Man-like Apes.	Chimpanzee.
11. Old World Monkey.	Dumb Apes.	What is it ?
12. MAN.	MAN.	MAN.

APPENDIX S, PAGE 191.

To show how widely the speculative school differ among themselves respecting Egyptian history when they ignore Scripture, I quote the following instances as the conclusions of distinguished Egyptologers :—

1. Mariette dates the era of Menes, B.C., 5004.
2. Brugsch ,, ,, ,, ,, 4400.
3. Lepsius ,, ,, ,, ,, 3890.
4. Bunsen ,, ,, ,, ,, 3059.

Showing a difference of 2000 years !

So as regards the sojourn of the Israelites in Egypt :—

1. Bunsen computes it at 1434 years.
2. Brugsch ,, ,, 400 ,,
3. Lepsius ,, ,, 90 ,,

While Scripture teaches from the time of God making a covenant with Abraham to the Exodus was exactly 430 years to a day; half of which time, or 215 years, the children of Israel were in Egypt. See Exodus xii. 40; Galatians iii. 16, 17.

APPENDIX T, PAGE 197.

A work which appeared in 1878, entitled, *A*

Hundred Wonders of the World in Nature and Art, by
John Small, M.A., will give an idea of the teaching
of that age by those who asserted strongly, reasoned
feebly, and quietly ignored the unerring Word of
Truth. "It is now *proved* that man has existed on
earth since a very remote period. Written documents
do not carry us back further than 6000 years. But
far beyond this short historic period extends a space
of time certainly much longer known to us only by
pure tradition......As we are *necessarily in doubt as to
the very origin of mankind*, it is obviously *impossible* to
ascertain whether the different races of the earth are
descended from *one couple*, or from several primitive
groups......Whatever may have been man's origin,
savagery is evidently the primitive condition of the
human race." Of these very large statements proceeding from a very "Small" man, we can only
deny every one of them. There is no "proof,"
though much speculation, as we have pointed out in
the text, for the high antiquity of man; and not a
shred of "pure tradition" for the same. The man
who believes God's Word has not a shadow of doubt
respecting the "origin of man" or the "unity of
race." And as for man being originally a "savage,"
it is so ludicrously contrary to all evidence, that
we may be content with a simple contradiction. Mr.
Small's rash sayings remind us of what once occurred
at a meeting of the Academy of Sciences in Paris,
May 1857, when M. le Baron Dupin informed the
public that "Omar, Mahomet's general, having
conquered the valley of the Nile, his lieutenant
suggested to him the formation of a canal direct
from Suez to Pelusium; but," continues the learned

Baron, "was it likely that Amrou, who was guilty of burning the Alexandrian library, should possess sufficient capacity to carry out so grand an idea?"

Now there are in this speech almost as many errors as words—1. Mahomet was dead when the Saracens invaded Egypt. 2. Omar did not conquer the valley of the Nile. 3. The canal from Suez to Pelusium. had existed for centuries. 4. Amrou did not burn the Alexandrian library, seeing that it had been destroyed two and a half centuries before.

APPENDIX U, PAGE 201.

The *Edinburgh Review* of April, 1873, draws a very powerful contrast between Mr. Darwin's *Expression of the Emotions in Man and Animals*, and Sir Charles Bell's *Anatomy and Philosophy of Expression in Connexion with the Fine Arts*, very much in favour of the latter. I have recently had an opportunity of reading these two works of such distinguished writers in sequence to each other, and can readily add my testimony in support of the justice of the reviewer's verdict. "With regard to style and treatment," says the *Edinburgh*, "Sir Charles Bell was not more decisively Mr. Darwin's superior as an anatomist and physiologist than as a man of taste, and of literary and philosophical culture. His style is marked by the rarest union of gracefulness and strength, of purity, precision, and admirably co-ordinated scientific and literary power. On the other hand, Mr. Darwin's writing is marked by slang phrases, vulgarisms, and a pervading looseness of

268 APPENDICES.

structure, that, apart from the interest of the subject, would often make the mere reading a wearisome task. We only wish there were space at command to exemplify Sir Charles Bell's immense superiority in this respect. But all who are familiar with his Essay, will remember how happily it illustrates the higher culture that illuminates special knowledge, connects science with history and philosophy, and thus gives to its expositions a distinctively literary character, and a broadly human interest " (p. 500, &c).

APPENDIX V, PAGE 210.

That Book of Books which has satisfied the giant intellects of such men as Bacon, Milton, and Newton, is not likely to be overthrown, or in the slightest degree injured, by the puny efforts of such men as Professor Lesley of America, the late Bishop Colenso of Natal, or the writers of the *Westminster Review*, the chief organ of infidelity in England of the present day. When Bishop Colenso, misled by the ignorant remark of a savage from Zululand, commenced his onslaught on the Bible, and declared with astounding folly that Moses' story of the Exodus had no more historical truth in it than the assertion that two and two made five, nothing could exceed the contempt and scorn which cultured Jewish writers manifested for his daring blunders, and ludicrous attempts at Biblical criticism; and though it gave this unhappy Bishop a little notoriety at the time, I do not think it has disturbed a single Christian mind in the slightest degree. And how deeply the

Westminster Review, which gave Bishop Colenso its warm support, has been imbued with infidelity of the worst type during the last 20 years, we may judge by the following attack which it once made on the subject of Holy Scripture:—"It must never be forgotten, that the most monstrous of Christian superstitions, the most grotesque of Christian miracles, and the most inhuman of Christian dogmas, find their prototype in the books of the Old and New Testament, that medley of documents, which, with much that is true, pathetic and sublime, *contains not a little that is false, inhuman and immoral,*" (*W.R.*, October 1865, p. 350). What the late lamented Duke of Albany said at the Tait Memorial Meeting in 1883 concerning "that false opposition between reason and revelation (so prevalent in the present day), as though in this world of awful mysteries, a spirit of arrogant irreverence were not the very maddest unreason,"—is peculiarly applicable to this self-sufficient infidel writer of the *Westminster Review*, who has thus, in the pride of an unsanctified intellect, endeavoured most falsely to disparage the infallible Word of God. Revelation xxii. 7, 14, 15, 18, 19.

APPENDIX W, PAGE 221.

Possibly Mr. Darwin may have been evolved from the author of *Hamlet*, and was reminded of his celebrated ancestor's theory, when he explained in the *first* edition of his *Origin of Species* how a bear might evolve a whale, as Hamlet is represented as asking—

" Do you see yonder cloud, that's almost in shape of a camel ? "

Polonius.—" By the mass, and 'tis like a camel, indeed."

Hamlet.—" Methinks it is like a weasel."

Polonius.—" It is backed like a weasel."

Hamlet.—" Or like a whale ? "

Polonius.—" Very like a whale." (Act iii., scene 2.)

ERRATA.

Page 26, line 4, *for* " Aquileius " *read* " Apuleius."

 ,,   76, ,,   4, ,, " Lord Monboddo's " *read* " Lord Monboddo."

Page 77, line 5, *for* " Salmaneser " *read* " Shalmaneser."

Page 88, line 21, *for* " monod " *read* " monad."

www.ingramcontent.com/pod-product-compliance
Lightning Source LLC
Chambersburg PA
CBHW021219270326
41929CB00010B/1188